MUSIC
AND
LITURGY

CLAUDE DUCHESNEAU
MICHEL VEUTHEY

MUSIC
AND
LITURGY

*The Universa Laus Document
and Commentary*

Translated
—— By ——
Paul Inwood

The Pastoral Press
Washington, DC

Originally published as *Musique et Liturgie* by Les Editions du Cerf, Paris. Copyright © 1988, Les Editions du Cerf.

English translation copyright © 1992, Paul Inwood and The Pastoral Press.

ISBN: 0912405-98-8

The Pastoral Press
225 Sheridan Street, N.W.
Washington, D.C. 20011
(202) 723-1254

The Pastoral Press is the publications division of the National Association of Pastoral Musicians, a membership organization of musicians and clergy dedicated to fostering the art of musical liturgy.

Printed in the United States of America

This book was produced
under the supervision of

CLAUDE DUCHESNEAU

with the collaboration of
MICHEL VEUTHEY
(for the main commentary)

and
(for the technical notes)

JEAN BIHAN
JEAN-CLAUDE CRIVELLI
MICHEL CORSI
JEAN EVENOU
PIERRE FAURE
JOSEPH GELINEAU
MARIE-JOSETTE GERN
JEAN LEBON
DIDIER RIMAUD
GINO STEFANI

For the English-language edition:

additional material by

VIRGIL C. FUNK
PAUL INWOOD

Contents

Introduction
The "Universa Laus" Group

Universa Laus, an "international group for the study of singing and instrumental music[1] in the liturgy," was officially born in Lugano, Switzerland, in April 1966. However, a number of those who were present on the day the group was founded had already been working together for many years. In some cases they were doing so as private individuals, in others through affiliation with the groups running journals such as *Musik und Altar* in Germany (Erhard Quack and Helmut Hucke) or *Eglise qui chante*, the publication of the Association Saint-Ambroise "for promoting the singing of the people" which had been founded in France in 1957 by David Julien, René Reboud, Lucien Deiss, and Joseph Gelineau.

When the Second Vatican Council was announced, and when it became clear that a first priority in its work would be a "Constitution on the Liturgy," these same liturgists and musicologists undertook to support the work of those whose task it was to present texts and schemas to the Council Fathers. This work of support began with the group's very first meeting at Crésus in Switzerland in 1962, and continued right up to the Fribourg meeting of 1965 when a complete panorama of the role of instrumental music and singing in the reform of the Roman liturgy was presented under the title *Le Chant liturgique après Vatican II*. This milestone in liturgical musicology was published in five languages. It opened up the possibility of tackling questions arising

---

1. French differentiates between *chant* (singing) and *musique* (instrumental music), but also uses *musique* to mean music in the more general sense. This differentiation is maintained in this book by using the word "instrumental" whenever necessary [translator's note].

from different points of view: historical, theological, technical, and pastoral. From this era dates the faithful friendship for *Universa Laus* of Msgr. Annibale Bugnini, who was unstinting in his encouragement and support of the group's work.

The years that followed saw the implementation of the reforms of Vatican II. At that time *Universa Laus* was alternating two types of meetings: working sessions most years, and congresses of a more open kind (Essen, Pamplona, Turin, Amsterdam, Strasbourg, etc) from time to time. During this period numerous publications appeared as the fruit of *Universa Laus'* work.[2]

These years also saw a rapid change in the landscape. At the same time as liturgical music was proliferating across many countries in new vernacular versions of Roman Catholic rites, a new era was opening up: the encounter between worship and culture.

Up to this point, the main thrust of the group's work had been the study of the "ritual function" of liturgical chants. It was becoming increasingly clear that a study of the effective "functioning" of these same chants would also have to be undertaken. As a result, the group turned its attention to the fields of human behavior, social customs, and cultural differences. The exchanges between members from different countries became less easy than when these members had been discussing history or theology. From this point on, it was necessary to have recourse to sciences such as semiology, cultural anthropology, and socio-psychology, areas less familiar to the group and which remained rather more delicate to deal with in the context of signs of faith. Nevertheless, some guidelines were proposed. Gino Stefani's book *L'Acclamation de tout un peuple*, published in 1967, produced a working *credo*: every act of singing is a "vocal gesture" which possesses both bodily roots and a socio-cultural environment. From that moment on, a new trilogy became inevitable: Music - Rite - Culture.

In a new context of flexible liturgical practice, and in the light of the great diversity of presentations and interpretations produced by the conjunction of those three words, was it still possible for

---

2. In France, volumes appeared in the "Kinnor" collection published by Editions Fleurus, and special numbers of the magazine *Eglise qui chante* carried articles. In English, articles can be found in the journals *Church Music* and its successor *Music and Liturgy*.

Universa Laus to venture to make public its thoughts as a group? Many people were asking this question. Wasn't it the right time to bring together the fruit of a quarter of a century of reflection and research, not in a unified and closed doctrinal *corpus* but rather in the form of a "manifesto"? This would also provide a document that could serve as a point of reference, pointing out different "lines of force" and attempting to define a number of useful concepts.

In 1977, during a meeting at Gentinnes, Belgium, it was decided to embark on this project. Three years later, the members of *Universa Laus* were presented with the "1980 *Universa Laus* document," entitled *De la musique dans les liturgies chrétiennes.*

This document comprised two sections:

> I— Points of Reference, an "organically arranged" presentation in ten chapters;
>
> II— Beliefs Held in Common, consisting of forty-five aphorisms which present the same content in a more incisive and perhaps more stimulating form.

Once the *Universa Laus* document had been published in the various languages of the group, it could be used according to the different musical, ecclesial, cultural, and pastoral situations obtaining in each country. The French-speaking group decided to work toward a book that would follow the organization of material in the document and utilize the great wealth of that material. This book would be offered to anyone interested in Christian music in worship, whether they be composers, pastors, choir directors, animators, or simply those wanting a solid and broad base of data and material for reflection.

The present volume is a translation, adapted for the English-speaking world, of the French book. A more detailed history of the formation of the document itself follows below.

SHORT HISTORY OF THE DOCUMENT

Scarcely three years after the publication of the conciliar constitution *Sacrosanctum Concilium*, the association known as *Universa Laus* was established at Lugano in April 1966. Because the founding members were among those who had prepared for the conciliar reforms, they naturally wanted to promote the study of singing and instrumental music in the liturgy according to the spirit of Vatican II. The work produced by this research group was marked by two principal characteristics: it was firmly rooted in tradition—and hence in time—and it was international.

Pius X's motu proprio *Tra le sollecitudini* of 1903 had given the concepts of the Caecilian movement official status. These concepts were a reaction against music of an operatic type: their rationale was the promotion of ancient music. In his encyclical *Mediator Dei* of 1947, Pius XII perceived the importance of (under certain conditions) not severing sacred music from the potential contribution of the surrounding musical culture, and in his 1955 encyclical *Musicae Sacrae Disciplina* made a place for popular religious song. This place was confirmed—and not without certain restrictions— by the instruction *Musica Sacra et Sacra Liturgia* issued by the Congregation of Rites in 1958.

In its turn, the council proved sensitive to the musicological problem, but the conciliar constitution *Sacrosanctum Concilium* of 1963 was still pervaded by a vocabulary possessing juridical and aesthetic overtones. To give it its full scope, it is necessary to read this constitution in the light of the complete body of conciliar documents, together with the 1967 instruction *Musicam Sacram* issued by the Congregation of Rites and the Concilium.

The focus was changed: the liturgical mystery and the people involved in the action of celebrating are the point of departure for all research. The liturgy is a celebration: in liturgy singing and instrumental music have sacramental weight. Repertoires and instruments must allow assemblies living in their particular cultures to express themselves authentically when celebrating. This is the area in which *Universa Laus* has been working.

After eleven years of work and regular meetings, the idea of a *Universa Laus* document was born in Gentinnes, Belgium, in August 1977, as already mentioned above. Despite a large-scale agreement of perspective on a number of subjects, some were afraid that it would not prove possible to arrive at a final text that everyone could agree upon, let alone disseminate more widely— and this for reasons of basic principles as well as how those principles might be expressed. Nevertheless the discussions led to the idea of producing a long document (in fact a book) based on beliefs which were supposed to be held in common, from which a short document (a sort of charter) would later on be extracted. A number of *Universa Laus* members would be invited to provide contributions with this in mind.

In March 1978 in Luxembourg, after the requested contributions had been distributed and studied, the project was changed: the short text would be produced first. This would enable the group to select more carefully those to whom the document would be given (first of all, *Universa Laus* members and people working in liturgy, rather than the general public); it would also enable the group to produce a text having a prophetic character, rather than a dogmatic and doctrinaire declaration. Its content would have to acknowledge the state of tension between creativity and regimentation, propose pathways for research, and emphasize the urgency of the formation of liturgical animators and the future role of *Universa Laus*. Claude Duchesneau was asked to produce a series of "theses" with commentaries.

In London in August 1978, Duchesneau's work presented the context in which *Universa Laus'* thought was situated. It was organized under six main headings. Joseph Gelineau took this text, put it into a more general framework, and re-organized it into "theses" followed by a general commentary. At the end of the congress, the organization's Praesidium read and discussed this latter text, and approved it for translation and discussion by the different language groups.

In October, after the various national groups had reviewed it, it became clear that, in addition to adaptations necessary from the point of view of translation, a reworking of the text would also be necessary.

Critiques were sent to Michel Veuthey at the beginning of 1979. They can be summarized as follows: text too abstract, language too specialized, a great emphasis on a theory of communication, not enough emphasis on theological aspects. In general, the groups belonging to non-Latin cultures felt constricted by the structure of concepts and lines of thought underpinning the text.

In March 1979 the Praesidium met in Paris, examined the criticisms, and decided not just on corrections but on a complete reworking of the document.

In June 1979 Joseph Gelineau submitted a second text. It is more or less the one found in this book. This text was examined again during the working meeting at Candia (in the Canavese region of Italy) in the same year, and final corrections were made. It was a shorter text with a larger number of chapters. The language was less technical; and the original "theses" had become "beliefs held in common," placed after the ten chapters containing "points of reference." This text was offered to members of *Universa Laus* for approval at Assisi in August 1980.

Since then the group has continued its work and its annual meetings in different European countries—St. Maurice (Switzerland), Walbourg (France), Gazzada (Italy), Paderborn (Germany), Aix-en-Provence (France), Capiago-Lugano (Italy), Waterloo (Belgium), Montserrat (Spain), Worth (England), Altenberg (Germany), and Innsbruck (Austria).[3] However, the planned longer document discussed in Gentinnes and Luxembourg remained pending until 1988, when the present book was published in French. Its intention is, therefore, to be that longer document.

One might ask what purpose is served by including the original document here: after all, it was completed more than ten years ago. The answer is quite simple: this document continues to provide avenues for research for *Universa Laus*; it serves as a point of reference for the group, or better still, a springboard. Extracts from it are often used during formation courses for liturgical animators, as a point of departure for reflection in common. The three-pronged basis for research of "Culture-Music-Liturgy" is still full of possibilities.

The *Universa Laus* document is characterized by its density, its manifesto-type form, and the diversity of cultures and formation of its authors. These characteristics, as well as being qualities, are also limitations. To make the document accessible to everyone, the seedbed from which it was developed needs to be brought to light again. The point-by-point commentary by Michel Veuthey, General Secretary of *Universa Laus* from its foundation, fulfills this function. In order to keep it readable and also useful as a working instrument, this commentary has recourse to technical notes (appearing as a Glossary[4] in this translation). These have been produced by a group of collaborators from French-speaking countries.[5]

---

3. List correct up to 1991.
4. Abbreviated as GL in this book.
5. These notes have been left relatively unchanged for the English-language edition as they are of considerable interest. A little additional material has been added where necessary.

For whom is this book intended? Everyone involved with singing and instrumental music in Christian worship: authors of texts, composers, professional musicians, liturgists, people with pastoral responsibility, people involved in formation, and the vast numbers of those who regularly help their assemblies to find a voice.

The *Universa Laus* document is a fruit, growing on the tree of tradition, ripened in the course of lengthy research and the addressing of key issues. May it, in turn, bear fruit a hundredfold.

Part One

The Document

"Music in Christian Celebration"

Foreword [1]

In 1962 a group of liturgical musicians came together to study and discuss the theory and practice of Christian liturgical music. This group expanded rapidly, and formally constituted itself as *Universa Laus* ("Universal Praise") in 1966. Its membership is worldwide, though firmly based in Europe at present; it is primarily Roman Catholic, but other denominations are represented and welcomed; it has a healthy mixture of clergy and laity. All kinds of people—from learned academic liturgists and musicologists to grass-roots pastors and musicians—are involved in *Universa Laus*. What unites them is that they have all, to a greater or lesser extent, thought about liturgical music. The common desire animating them is to understand ever more clearly and ever more deeply how liturgy works and how music works within liturgy.

---

1. This is a modified form of the introduction to the document published in the journal *Music and Liturgy*, Summer 1980, vol. 8, nos. 3 / 4, pp. 151-2, and is an expansion of the prologue contained in the French original. The original draft of this English-language introduction was the work of Kevin Donovan S.J., at that time one of the three Presidents of *Universa Laus*. The draft was heavily expanded by Paul Inwood, at that time General Editor of the journal *Music and Liturgy*. Because the document was originally "free-standing," there is a small amount of repetition of material already presented in the preceding pages of this book.

The text of the document itself largely follows the same issue of *Music and Liturgy*, pp. 152-161, but some minor corrections have been introduced. In addition, modifications have been made in the light of progress in the area of inclusive language.

Today, *Universa Laus* is an independent body for research into, and reflection on, liturgical music; and it is based on a strong foundation of international friendship, mutual respect, and the free exchange of ideas.

The first period in the group's existence (1962-1968) corresponded to the years when the Roman Catholic Church was creating and developing the liturgical reform that was the fruit of the Second Vatican Council. During this time *Universa Laus* carried out a program of research on singing and instrumental music in Christian worship. This program included historical, theological, technical, and pastoral aspects; and, through individual *Universa Laus* members well-placed to make a contribution, some of its results bore fruit in the reforms themselves.

The second period in the life of *Universa Laus* (1969-1976) was characterized by two new major influences. The first was the fact that, in the wake of the liturgical reforms, worship and culture had now begun to encounter each other; in different language-areas and different cultures this encounter had widely differing results. The second was cross-fertilization, similar to what was happening in most academic disciplines. In this case, new light was being shed on the study of ritual and music by contributions from other areas of the humanities, such as semiology, linguistics, social psychology, and anthropology. During this period, too, *Universa Laus* exerted an unseen but large influence on the implementation of the liturgical reforms and their subsequent development, mainly through the writings and teachings of some of its more prominent members.

By now it was evident that there was a growing divergence of cultural and ecclesial situations in the post-Vatican II world; and *Universa Laus* felt the need to question itself again about the beliefs and convictions of its members. Thus in 1977 was born the idea of a document—a statement which would set down a certain number of basic lines of thought common to the group, growing out of what they had learned during the previous fifteen years. After four years of discussion and a gradual refining process, *Universa Laus* is proposing the document given below; it hopes that its members will feel able to subscribe to it.

Like any précis, this document tries to synthesize a vast amount of work in a very small space. It is impossible to compress a year or two's work in one area into a single paragraph giving only the bare outline of the conclusion reached; and yet this is what is attempted here. The first part of the document—"Points of Reference"—is a trial presentation, arranged "organically," of the way in which *Universa Laus* views the relationships between music and Christian liturgy in 1980. The second part of the document— "Beliefs Held in Common"—takes up the points of reference and reworks them in the form of a series of brief statements.

Cultural divergence is mentioned or implied throughout the document, and it should be noted that there is always a difficulty in reproducing "international nuances" in an undertaking of this kind. The basic work was done by French-, German-, Italian- and English-speaking working-groups; and there are often problems in reproducing in one language the exact shade of meaning implicit in a word or phrase in another language. This applies particularly, though not exclusively, to words that have a certain technical meaning. There are some phrases in some languages that are literally untranslatable, and paraphrase has to be resorted to in such instances. In English, an additional complicating factor is the difference in modes of expression on either side of the Atlantic.[2]

---

2. Two English-language versions of the document have been published: the English version (in *Music and Liturgy,* already cited in footnote 1) and the American version (published in booklet form by the National Association of Pastoral Musicians). These freely drew upon each other's drafts. The English version has been used as the basis of the present translation.

Points of Reference

1. Singing in Christian Assemblies

1.1   The liturgy, namely the communal action of a people who gather together in the name of Jesus to celebrate the mysteries of their faith, is made up of a number of symbolic practices: rites and sacraments. Music has a special place among such practices.

1.2   Christian worship consists of:
   (a) the proclamation of salvation in Jesus Christ;
   (b) the response by the assembly of believers;
   (c) the making-real, by action, of the Covenant between God and humankind.

Music is integrated into these different components of worship:
   (a) to support and reinforce the proclamation of the Gospel in all its forms;
   (b) to give fuller expression to professing one's faith, to prayer (intercession), and to the giving of thanks;
   (c) to enhance the sacramental rite in its dual aspect of action and word.

1.3   The vocal and instrumental practices integral to Christian liturgy can be called by many names. Common expressions such as "sacred music," "religious music," or "church music" have broad and rather nebulous meanings which do not necessarily relate to the liturgy at all. Even the expression "liturgical music" (in the United States "musical liturgy") may not be precise enough to denote the unique relationship between liturgy and music that we are talking about here. Throughout the remainder of this document, therefore, we shall use the expression "(Christian) ritual music."

1.4 We understand "ritual music" to mean any vocal or instrumental practice which, in the context of celebration, diverges from the usual forms of the spoken word on the one hand and ordinary sounds on the other. The domain of sound that we have just defined can go beyond what certain cultural contexts would currently describe as "music" or "singing."

2. Christian Ritual Music in Various Cultures

2.1 In the same way that the languages and symbols used in Christian worship are or have been borrowed from the cultures in which the gospel message is or has been proclaimed, so Christian ritual music has developed and continues to develop according to the vocal and instrumental traditions of the groups of people where the liturgy is celebrated.

2.2 Although in the course of history different churches have developed repertoires that they considered as their own property, there is in fact no type of music as such that is specifically for Christian liturgy.

2.3 Nevertheless, we can see that Christian assemblies use different types of music in ways that are, to a greater or lesser extent, peculiar to them. The vocal or instrumental practices of these assemblies are integrated into an action whose goal is to make manifest the ever-new reality of salvation in Jesus Christ. These practices cannot be considered merely as a product of the surrounding culture. Liturgical practice is continually being questioned and challenged by the gospel experience which is at one and the same time memorial, conversion, and waiting for the coming of the Kingdom. These "evangelical aspects" (past, present, future hope) cannot, however, be isolated from the cultural forms they affect.

2.4 Christian ritual music has two principal characteristics:

(i) like liturgy itself, musical practice in liturgy is essentially something communal;

(ii) words play a specific part in it.

2.5   Dealing with types of music from various groups of people, Christian ritual music always works through a process of choices and transformations.

2.6   Not all the musical practices of a given culture are equally available to, or usable in, the liturgy. Divergences can be seen, not only with regard to non-religious or non-Christian types of music, but also—depending on the time and place of one's viewpoint—with regard to types of Christian "sacred music" belonging to other eras and cultures.

2.7   The other side of the coin is that liturgical celebration can welcome or require practices which the surrounding culture has no knowledge of or has allowed to atrophy.

2.8   Liturgical celebration is a symbolic whole; and all its elements, musical or not, are interdependent. Ritual music can therefore not be isolated from those other areas of culture which also have a bearing on the celebration: building-materials and architecture, the places where people gather together, language and poetry, gesture and dance, musical instruments, etc.

3. Singers and Musicians

3.1   In the liturgy, music, like all other ritual activity, must first be thought of in terms of the people who are celebrating.

3.2   The liturgical action is the action of an "assembly" of people gathered together at a single time and in a single place. Every word, everything that is sung, all the music that is played in the assembly, is the concern of each and everyone. Whether a rite is carried out by one individual, or by a few people, or by everyone together, it is always a communal action.

3.3   The distribution of vocal and instrumental tasks in Christian assemblies has varied greatly according to era and locality. These variations are due to various kinds of factors. The division of roles between people and ministers can be partly explained by the way in which the organic and hierarchic nature of the Christian assembly is understood, as well as by the sacred character of the liturgical action. But we also find here a reflection of social customs, according to which singing in public could be the task of an individual (whether man or woman), or of a group, or of everyone, depending on just as many different ways of listening and participating. The involvement of soloists, choirs, and instrumentalists is the result of evolution in musical techniques and an increase in the amount of available repertoire.

3.4   However, being of service to others in liturgy is never simply a matter of technical competence or social status. The participants' faith rests on the reality that every action, whether by one or several people, is taken as a sign of the action of the Holy Spirit in the group. So, in terms of the diaconal (or "service") role and the charisms (or "gifts of the Spirit") mentioned in the New Testament, liturgical roles are also considered as "ministries"—whether these ministers act by virtue of ordination, permanent institution, or occasional assignment.

3.5   The distribution of musical roles in the liturgy has greatly varied in the past and will undoubtedly vary much more in the future. Without prejudging any of these or wishing to be exhaustive in any way, we can nevertheless identify the following: the role of the people gathered together to worship; the roles of the individual ministers (presider, deacon, psalmist, cantor, etc.); the role of specialized groups (unison choir, schola, larger choir); and the role of instrumentalists. The roles of composers and planners/organizers of a celebration should also be added.

3.6   Singing by the people gathered together is highest in importance, and we can never dispense with it. Even in the absence of singing ministers and groups of singers, it is first and foremost the task of the assembly to profess its faith, in response to the proclaimed word of God, through "hymns, psalms, and spiritual songs" (Col 3:16). The musical role of others who might contribute will depend on the ability of the celebrating group to provide itself with such performers, as well as the style of celebration required by the group.

4. Music for Everyone

4.1   The music performed in an assembly is offered to the assembly as a symbolic sign of what the assembly is celebrating. But music, as a rite in itself, is also a task to be accomplished. In order fully to carry out its role, this music should be accessible to all who participate, both those who perform the music and those who listen to it.

4.2   The ritual music currently in use most often belongs to the "common practice" of the surrounding society, in the sense that this music does not require special musical skills and is thus accessible to the whole body of participants. This is normally the case whenever the entire assembly sings. But it is also true when ministers other than those in charge of the music—such as the priest, deacon, reader, or animator—are required to sing by themselves during a celebration.

4.3   A celebration can, nevertheless, be enriched by various more or less "specialized" musical practices if the necessary resources (soloists, choirs, instrumentalists) are available and if the overall plan of the celebration warrants these resources. This type of music is for listening to by the other participants. The way in which those other participants are affected will depend on whether the music has words or not, whether the music has been programmed to be listened to (without anything else going on simultaneously) or to provide an environment of sound for the rites, and whether it is close to or distant from the musical competence of the listeners. Whatever the case may be, it is to be expected that the music should make a contribution that is seen to be positive by the assembly. This is still possible even when the music deviates from what the listeners are accustomed to hearing.

4.4   It is appropriate for societies that enjoy a thriving traditional musical culture to make use of this culture in ritual practice, whether communal or specialized. On the other hand, a certain pluralism often seems necessary today in situations where the culture is mixed or fragmented; otherwise we risk favoring certain social milieux or categories of people at the expense of others.

5. Word and Singing

5.1 Just as Jewish liturgy proclaims the wonders of God and gives God thanks for them, so Christian liturgy has consisted of praise since the very beginning. Singing is in the very bones of Christian ritual as a medium for the Good News of salvation and the praise of a redeemed people. Bonded to the biblical and sacramental word, singing is the primary point of departure for Christian ritual music.

5.2 The word "singing" is used here in a broad sense to indicate many different kinds of vocal expressions. Its span ranges from practices like recitative to melismatic singing, including "song" in the usual sense of the word.

5.3 Liturgical celebration calls for a wide variety of vocal acts and verbo-musical genres because different functions of language are brought into play. Depending on the literary genre of the texts used, and above all on the relationship that it establishes between the participants, celebration sometimes emphasizes the transmission of a message, sometimes the savoring or assimilation of recited words, sometimes the act of singing "with one voice," sometimes pure praise for its own sake. Each of these types of language corresponds to a different relationship between text and music. In each case the group has its own special way of making the word its own.

5.4 Because the word of revelation is essential to Christian worship, the liturgy has, from its very beginnings, emphasized the function of verbal communication (of messages destined for the intelligence) (1 Cor 14:15). Safeguarding this priority in no way excludes other functions of language (such as relational function, function of awakening the heart, poetic function, etc.). It is often in these other functions of language that music has its most specific role.

5.5 Singing is not the result of bringing together music and text; nor is it the occasional encounter between pure music and pure poetry. It is an original human action in which words and sounds become a new, single unity. In singing, a text can take on meanings suggested by the music that goes with it, while the music can endlessly enlarge on the meaning of the words. Thanks to language, music can articulate the name of the God of Jesus Christ; through music, the human voice can attempt to utter the unutterable.

6. Music and Instruments

6.1 The special place assigned to singing in the liturgy as words bonded to music does not exclude the use of music without words, whether this music be vocal or instrumental, whether produced by traditional instruments or by electronic synthesizers, or reproduced by mechanical means.

6.2 For quite a long period of its history—and it is still true today in certain eastern rites—Christian tradition removed musical instruments from the liturgy. The social and religious motives behind this rejection have not entirely disappeared in all places. Nevertheless, instrumental music today constitutes in many societies a human and spiritual value whose contribution to Christian worship is now recognized as being a positive one.

6.3 One fact is obvious: in most cultures the act of singing, whether individually or collectively, integrates the use of accompaniment or performance instruments. These lend contrast to rhythm, melody, timbre, and words. They help the cohesion of the ensemble and influence the meaning that can be transmitted.

6.4 In certain cases, a musical act may constitute a rite in itself: e.g., the ringing of bells or music for meditation. In other cases it may be integral to a rite: e.g., a procession or an action without singing. Music can turn a moment into an event; music can give a certain quality to the passage of time in celebration, can signify a feast, can assist in contemplation, and in the end can itself become an act of prayer.

6.5 Making music together implies that each performer, to the best of his or her ability, will enter into what the whole group is doing. It is, therefore, scarcely conceivable that instrumentalists should bring nothing but technical competence to a celebration, without themselves being committed to the celebrating group of believers.

In the same way, composers will be able to place themselves fully at the service of the assemblies for which they write if they participate in the liturgies of these assemblies by listening to the word and responding to it in such a way as to discover in themselves the appropriate ways for the group to express its faith.

7. Ritual Functions

7.1   In liturgy, music fulfills a certain number of anthropological functions that relate to both the individual and the group. These are the same as those encountered in society as a whole. Some are general: the use of music for emotional expression, group solidarity, symbolizing festivity, etc. Others are more specialized: therapeutic, educational, recreational, etc. But inasmuch as music is a part of Christian celebration as such, it plays a specific role and fulfills a certain number of functions that are proper to itself.

7.2   These ritual functions fall into two main categories. Those in the first category are defined, in the sense that particular effects, more or less controllable, are intended. Those in the second category are indeterminate, with their effects being largely unpredictable.

7.3   Defined functions are principally the concern of people responsible for a celebration: composers, planners and organizers, implementers. Indeed, whether a celebration works well or not depends on these functions. In the same way that some kinds of music are good or bad for dancing, relaxation, choral singing, private enjoyment, etc., so in the liturgy there are kinds of music that are good or not so good for various functions of the word—proclaiming, meditating, psalm-singing, praise, acclamation, dialogue, response, etc.—and those that are useful or not so useful for different ritual moments: opening, processions, litanic supplication, and so on.

To each function correspond different musical forms, developed or selected in such a way as to make the rite as meaningful and effective as possible.

7.4   However, the role of music in the liturgy extends well beyond what one can see of how well it works. Like every symbolic sign, music "refers" to something beyond itself. It opens the door to the indefinable realm of meanings and reactions. Taken in terms of faith, music for the believer becomes the *sacramentum* and the *mysterion* of the realities being celebrated.

7.5   These two categories of ritual function always imply one another. Ritual music, therefore, is never programmed for its own sake (e.g., purely as a game, or simply for aesthetic titillation, or as art for art's sake), nor merely for practical ends (educational, social, recreational, etc.), nor even just so that the rite may be accomplished. In the final analysis, ritual music is always aiming at whole human individuals and their free and unfettered encounter in the assembly of believers with the God of Jesus Christ.

8. Repertoires and Models

8.1   Like the liturgy itself, which is first and foremost an "act," ritual music consists in the first place of "making music" together. Thus each rite is a unique occurrence, and each liturgy is a once-only event.

8.2   Nevertheless, rite is also by nature repetition, memorial, and social custom. This is why ritual music cannot regularly bypass pre-existing works. This is the way repertoires of Christian ritual music have developed.

8.3   In celebration, different factors motivate the use of existing repertoires. The first level is primarily practical. For example, in order that a dialogue can be established between the presider and the assembly, or in order that the assembly can together sing an antiphon or a *Holy, holy,* words and music must already exist. Second, there can be aesthetic motivations: the most valuable works, those that are richest in meaning, are most valuable precisely because they exist in a finished form. We expect them to be performed in the form in which they exist. Third, celebration can be enriched by the emotional and intellectual connotations that certain works have gradually acquired according to the different experiences of various individuals and groups.

8.4   Despite the use of particular musical compositions that form part of one repertoire or another, there is a constant call in liturgy for the kind of music that is not easily reconciled with a completely fixed repertoire. The solo cantillation of a psalm or a preface, even making use of a given tone, allows the performer a certain latitude for improvisation that can benefit the transmission of the text. Again, some types of spontaneous polyphony are not susceptible to being written down on paper. In these and other cases a traditional technique is employed: a more or less regulated use of an "operative musical model."

8.5   The use of operative models allows the two aspects of ritual—repetition and newness—to work together. By taking well-known pathways and familiar routes, the use of the model facilitates the acceptance and the practice of a rite in a given cultural context. By allowing certain variations and innovations, the model can contribute to the unique event that each celebration actually is. The model also makes it possible to expand the repertoire without upsetting the participants through an excess of novelty.

8.6   The musical organization of a celebration can be inspired by two complementary principles: on the one hand, the use of well-known pieces, familiar and within the grasp of everyone, which are thereby good "tools for prayer"; on the other hand, the insertion at opportune moments of pieces with a more markedly aesthetic character, heard less often, rendered by competent performers, which will thereby be found to have acquired a special significance.

9. Quality and Value of Forms

9.1   When looking at the history of the churches—whether in regard to the interventions of authority or the behavior of the faithful—a constant twofold concern can be seen concerning ritual forms, and especially musical forms. The first aspect is expressed in terms such as "dignity," "beauty," "appropriateness," "good taste," "quality," "art," and so on. The other aspect has to do with the holiness of the action: the action is to be "prayerful" and "sacred."

9.2   When people demand "beauty" and "holiness" of liturgical forms, it is not so much a question of aesthetic or moral norms, Rather, it is a question of the "values" that a group of people are aiming at in their symbolic action and of the "anti-values" that the group considers incompatible with the rites. Detecting these values and anti-values, and discovering the tangible expressions through which they are perceived, turn our attention to the group's beliefs, spirituality, and faith, in addition to social psychology and to the status of art and religion in society.

9.3 Without claiming to have an exhaustive knowledge of the reactions of the faithful (reactions which are generally implicit rather than explicit, and which are usually badly-formulated), musicians who want to place themselves at the service of their assemblies cannot totally ignore nor neglect these reactions. It is useful for musicians, for example, to know which forms their people consider to be archaic, modern, or unfashionable; which they consider to be popular, elitist, or common; which are familiar or esoteric; which are good or bad in the view both of the experts and the "consumers"; which are sentimental or austere, prayerful or distracting, etc. It is also important to notice what proportion of the assembly expresses such reactions, and also to determine if such reactions are occasioned by the work itself or by the way in which it is performed.

9.4 The goal of those in charge of celebrations, as they seek to understand the effects of the musical forms they use, is not to adjust themselves to the taste of their public. They are delimiting the parameters within which the signs and rites of Christian faith can unfold. They notice to what extent different meanings are available or not. Then, in company with their fellow-believers, they search for the forms most suitable for celebrating in spirit and in truth.

9.5 Whatever the functions fulfilled by ritual music, whatever repertoire is used, and no matter how the pieces are performed, the way in which any particular type of music is perceived will always depend on the sonic "form" through which the music comes across to the members of the assembly. In this context, "form" includes not only the work, written down or improvised, but also its performance, taking into account the ability of the singers, the timbre of the voices, the acoustics of the place, and—not least—the celebration as a whole, of which the music in question is a part.

10. Signs of a New Humanity

10.1 The demands made by Christian ritual music spring from the ultimate goal of this music, which is to make manifest and make real a new humanity in the risen Jesus Christ. Its truth, worth, and grace are not only measured by its capacity to arouse active participation, nor by its aesthetic cultural value, nor its long history of acceptance in the church, nor by its popular success, but because it allows believers to cry out the *Kyrie eleisons* of the oppressed, to sing the *Alleluias* of those restored to life, and to uphold the *Maranatha* of the faithful in the hope of the coming of the Kingdom.

10.2 Any kind of music created by human beings can be of service to Christian worship, so long as it does not turn people in on themselves or merely reflect the image of themselves.

10.3 For centuries, certain cultures have sung the "new song" referred to in the Book of Psalms and the Book of Revelation, using innumerable different forms. Other peoples and continents are called to add their native arts to the service of this same act of praise. But many voices are still missing from the chorus of the 144,000 Elect (Rv 14:1-3). Some still have no voice with which to sing the new Canticle, not just in places where the Gospel has not yet been proclaimed but in places where it has not yet fully permeated humankind and human culture, and in other places where—though planted many ages ago—it must once again inspire a world in the full flood of being transformed.

Let there be *Universa Laus*—universal praise!

Beliefs Held in Common

1. Singing and instrumental music are a structural part of Christian liturgy.

2. It is not possible to be concerned with liturgy, either in theory or in practice, without taking music into account.

3. Those concerned with music in the liturgy must have both the rites and the people who celebrate as their point of reference.

4. Singing and instrumental music in the liturgy are at the service of the people gathered together to celebrate.

5. Ritual music always interacts with the cultural milieu in which it is used.

6. Not all musical practices in a given society lend themselves equally well to Christian celebration.

7. Certain musical practices, perfectly justifiable in a ritual context, may not be recognized by society as being musical art.

8. Christians do not possess a kind of music separate from other people; but they make use of each type of music in their own particular way.

9. No type of music is in itself profane, or sacred, or liturgical, or Christian; but there do exist types of ritual music in Christian worship.

10. In Christian worship, praise is first and foremost the task of all the people gathered together.

11. In celebration, even singing by one individual is the action of all.

12. For a particular assembly, there are many different ways of performing and listening to that assembly's ritual music.

13. Ritual music stems principally from musical practices held in common.

14. All musicians with a role in the celebration must acquire competence commensurate with their role.

15. The action of an assembly of believers can be rendered false by musicians who provide only a technical service without also associating themselves to the celebration.

16. The primary form of Christian ritual music is singing.

17. Singing is an original human act and is irreplaceable in celebration.

18. In liturgy, types of singing are just as varied as types of verbal acts.

19. Certain kinds of singing assume the use of musical instruments.

20. Music without words also has its place in liturgy.

21. Music is not indispensable to Christian liturgy, but its contribution is irreplaceable.

22. A celebration is a whole; and all of its elements—musical and non-musical—are interdependent.

23. When music takes place within a rite, it always affects both the form and the signifying power of the rite.

24. Ritual music can be described as "functional art."

25. In liturgy, singing and music fulfil a certain number of more or less defined functions.

26. As a symbolic sign, singing and music play a role above and beyond determined ritual functions.

27. A vocal or musical rite is first of all an event, a unique and singular act.

28. Liturgy is never "fully ripened"; it is always "developing."

29. Insofar as ritual music is a repetitive and collective act, it cannot do without repertoire altogether.

30. A good repertoire alone is not enough to guarantee that music will fulfil its liturgical role.

31. The performance of many musical rites benefits from the technique of the "operative model."

32. Experience is necessary to find out what is right for a particular assembly.

33. For liturgical celebration, good "musical tools" are needed first of all; it is also appropriate that works of musical art should enrich the signifying power of a celebration.

34. The wealth of meaning of a celebration is not proportionate to the amount of musical resources employed.

35. The use of different musical styles and genres in the same celebration is legitimate as long as it does not interfere with the unity of the ritual action but co-operates with it.

36. Communion between Christians of different assemblies, languages, cultures, and denominations can be expressed with the aid of a small number of common signs, among which music has a special place.

37. Everything that reaches the ears passes through the medium of an acoustic "form."

38. The effective functioning of every musical rite assumes the use of an appropriate form.

39. To be concerned with the form alone is idolatry; but to neglect the form is to neglect the rite.

40. There is a communal and constant demand for "beauty" and "holiness" with regard to liturgical forms. This has to do with the "values" that each group considers as essential.

41. Knowing the positive and negative judgments of the faithful on different types of music allows those in charge to make better use of these types in the liturgy.

42. Richness of meaning depends on the uniqueness of the signifying power of the form.

43. The goal of all Christian ritual music is to manifest and make real a new humanity in the risen Christ.

44. No musical practice is neutral in relationship to gospel faith.

45. The "new Canticle" will not be achieved until people of every race, language, and culture have joined their voices to it.

Part Two

Commentary on the Document

1

Singing in Christian Assemblies

For some years now, signs of a renewal have been on the increase in the Christian Churches. Almost everywhere there has been a development in biblical research, historical study, theological reflection, and liturgical experience. At a deeper level, pastoral and missionary endeavors have been seeking a more evangelical spirit, while a real spiritual thirst has shown itself at many levels among Christians.

To be sure, the fruits of this renewal are scarcely apparent to a superficial observer, since too many atrophied structures and closed minds continue to contribute to the maintaining of an image of a Christianity that is aging or even in its death throes. It is no less true that new forces are at work, and we would not want to make the mistake of seeing in them the action of the Spirit ever-present in a changing world.

Singing and instrumental music have no choice but to reflect this evolution. It was therefore not only right but indispensable for the members of the *Universa Laus* group to unite their efforts and their competencies in the cause of attempting to define the role and the place of musical elements in the liturgy.

An objection that might be raised is that these aspects of ecclesial life are only of secondary importance. Certainly the future of Christianity does not hinge upon them. But their very nature and their impact upon the senses allows them to play a role which shows up trends and differences of opinion. Singing and instrumental music, on the other hand, constitute a special means

of expressing faith. Under these two headings—senses and faith—
we would be wrong to neglect the tensions and problems that are
raised by singing and instrumental music.

To clarify this, it will be helpful first to ask ourselves about the
phenomenon itself: why do Christians sing during their celebrations?

Right from its very first paragraph, the *Universa Laus* document
affirms a basic principle: it describes singing and instrumental
music as being an integral part of the "symbolic practices" (GL 55,
p. 168) of the liturgy, and not simply exterior additions like icing
on the cake. This integration of singing and instrumental music as
elements of liturgy gives the document its own proper "color": far
from devaluing music or giving it a lower priority, the document
opens up for music a future rich with promise.

In fact, this way of conceiving the role of music in the liturgy
allows us to leave behind both the traditional concept of music
considered as a sign of "solemnity" (GL 53, p. 167) and the modern
concept of "fine arts" (GL 14, p. 124). This produces a link between
an anthropology and a theology at once more biblical and more
modern (GL 2, p. 114), notably in the rediscovery of the meaning
of the liturgical assembly and the relationships which are created
within this assembly.

Members of a human group always communicate by means of
perceivable signs, looks, gestures, spoken words . . . and so it is
naturally the same in Christian assemblies as their members
gather to celebrate. Communication between Christians in the
assembly—a communication which is the sign of their (real or at
least intentional) communion—necessarily takes place through
their gestures and their words. Gestures and words manifest and
reinforce the community, and in turn become signs of another
reality: the place of the mysterious encounter between God and
people, which is itself the object of Christian worship.

Musical elements form a part of these signs and, in this sense,
we now accord them a value and an importance which was
certainly not the case till quite recently. Many musicians, by failing
to understand this change of attitude, have for too long feared the
subjection of music to liturgy, seeing in this the basis for the
musician's submission to the liturgist. However, these musicians
are now gradually realizing that different forms of instrumental
music and singing are once again being endowed with a deeper

rationale, thanks to this closer link with the liturgical action. And this will certainly constitute the beginnings of a new vitality for all music destined for use in liturgy.

An enlightening analogy for this concept can be found in the history of architecture. At the end of the Middle Ages, when sculpture was escaping the confines of architecture—in other words, when sculptors created statues in their studios and later installed them in a building with a greater or lesser degree of success—the sculptor consciously rejoiced in an almost total freedom; but how the sculptor's work fits in with the edifice often remains problematical. It was the opposite in the preceding period, when the romanesque sculptors worked on site, fashioning walls, tympana, and column capitals: here, respect for the architectural form was a stimulus to the creative imagination. What might have appeared to be a limitation actually became a promise of unity for the work. At such periods sculpture benefits greatly from that intimate communion which seems to be lost when sculpture achieves independence. When sculpture gives itself up to the edifice, in return the edifice gives value to sculpture.

The same will apply when all our forms of music once more become living elements in liturgy; when the musician can work in collaboration and in communion with others responsible for the liturgy; when musicians really feel themselves to be actors in the celebration, linked to the whole of the gathered community. In this role, they will renounce the freedom to play whatever piece pleases them, but they will gain a feeling of being integrated into a real whole. For an artist, the unity of the work to be created—in its manifestation and in the ensemble of the liturgical action—will be a high priority.

MAIN AXES OF THE LITURGICAL ACTION

This concept immediately has important ramifications for church musicians, who can no longer present themselves simply with their musical "baggage"—their musical knowledge and competence. Just as an author who wants to write the libretto for an opera needs to know this art form and its requirements, so musicians who want to be involved in the service of the liturgy must know what liturgy is, must be familiar with the main axes of the celebration, must understand the elements with which their musical art has to take shape. We ought to add that the work of musicians will fit in all the better with the demands of the celebration when liturgists, for their part, take the trouble to acquaint themselves with the requests and resources of the musician—all of which will lead to a fruitful collaboration.

Without going into details on the rites at this point, it will be useful to recall the fundamental dimensions of liturgy:

1. God speaks to the gathered people. Through the reading of Scripture and through commentary on the texts of the liturgy of the word, God asks the people to adhere ever more closely to the Covenant. God invites them to re-present the actions of Jesus and to be united with each other in order to work at building up the Kingdom (GL 21, p. 129).

2. The assembly responds to the God of the Covenant through faith. It expresses wonder for the work of the Savior and thanksgiving for the marvels that he accomplishes. It acknowledges its own weakness and its confidence in grace. It reaffirms what it undertakes in relation to the needs of the world, undertakings to which every believer knows that he or she is invited to make a real contribution.

3. The members of the assembly accomplish certain symbolic gestures—first and foremost those of baptism by water and of eucharist by the sharing of bread and wine—thus translating into action their desire to keep to the Covenant which the Lord unceasingly offers to them.

MUSIC OPENS UP NEW DIMENSIONS

In each of these phases, singing and instrumental music can make their own contribution and become elements in the symbolic interplay accomplished in and by the assembly.

The Texts

The word of God is generally mediated in the form of spoken words, through the mouth of the presiding priest or a reader; but music in certain cases gives these words a new dimension.

In fact, the phrases of an ordinary text address themselves first of all to our intelligence. A poetic text already goes further than this, giving a new resonance to the words by the mysterious action of images, sonorities, and rhythms. A sung text develops this perception even more through the way in which musical rhythms, melodic movements, and the interplay of chords and variations in timbre amplify these textual resonances.

For example, cantillation (GL 7, p. 120), or sung performance, or an instrumental background, can emphasize the poetic character of a text because certain readings lend themselves to this sort of proclamation, one which goes beyond ordinary language. The lyrical nature of the eucharistic prayer also opens up musical possibilities. But the most notable instances of this type of text are found in the psalms and in the Old and New Testament canticles.

Indeed, music's action in such cases can be prolonged beyond the text itself, for instance when instrumental music underpins the silent meditation that is provoked by certain readings.

The Rites

Singing and instrumental music can also lead to a silence within which the Lord can speak to our hearts—hearts that are often overburdened with words and noise.

But singing and music also help to give value to certain gestures and certain rites—gestures of offering, rites of communion—sustaining the movement of a procession, creating a festive atmosphere or a mood of recollection, and even sometimes becoming rites in themselves, as we will see later (in Chapter 7).

The Assembly

It is true that a text is often better understood intellectually by those who utter it if it is simply spoken, rather than getting confused by music and its demands; but what a chant loses in intelligibility it regains for the most part through the affective and communal resonances that it evokes.

Sometimes the assembly speaks out the word through psalms and canticles: this way of responding reinforces the assembly's conviction and creates the right conditions for the message to be assimilated. In its desire for conversion expressed in the course of the penitential rite, and in the universal intercessions which follow the announcing of the word, the assembly's petitions can become more intense through singing. When the assembly has received the gifts of God in the sacrament, its hymns of thanksgiving translate its wonderment and its acknowledgement of what has happened better than any words could.

Through singing, the assembly above all develops an awareness of its own proper cohesion. This is especially important at the beginning of a celebration, when men and women coming from very different backgrounds are invited to form a worshiping community. But this force for communion is equally experienced at other moments—at times of intercession, in the profession of faith, in acclamations, in hymns of praise and thanksgiving, in chants where the assembly expresses its desire to be involved in the church at the service of the world.

SOME TERMINOLOGY

Having sketched out a rough picture of this integration of singing and instrumental music in a celebration, it is useful to refine a little further the terminology used in this area.

The normative texts of the churches—as with contemporary language, for that matter—use a number of terms to designate music performed in celebrations. If we are fairly indifferent as to which term is used, then the frequent use of one individual term can reveal a particular concept:

1. "Religious music" remains rather vague, and indicates any music born of a religious sentiment or composed from the starting-point of a religiously-inspired text.

2. "Church music" is close to "religious music" but, by specifying the place where this music is normally performed, the term includes connotations of volume of space and atmosphere (fullness, solemnity, etc.).

3. "Sacred music" is equally a general notion in the same sort of line as the two preceding terms, but here we can see that the aim is to establish a clear boundary with "profane" music.

4. "Liturgical music" turns our minds toward the use of music in the course of a celebration, and emphasizes the functional link between musical art and liturgy, at the same time distancing itself from an exclusively aesthetic conception of music.

5. "Ritual music" translates and underlines the deep union that we are seeking between a particular kind of music and the rite for which it has been composed, or selected, or performed (GL 46, p. 159).

6. "Pastoral music," a designation used in the United States, refers to music which is suitable for use at the parish level—including liturgy, religious education, social justice, and evangelization.

Even within a celebration the relationship between rite and music can vary a great deal. In particular, we should distinguish between music that constitutes a rite in itself—e.g., the singing of the *Sanctus* in the Roman rite—and music that accompanies a rite—e.g., a chant intended to accompany a procession.

This is why, in order to evoke the integration of music and rite already mentioned, the *Universa Laus* document prefers to speak of "Christian ritual music" or "music in Christian liturgies," neither of which confers any qualitative, aesthetic, formal, or historical judgment but simply insists on the music's essential function—i.e., its integration with the liturgy. To be even more precise but in a rather lengthier fashion, the document could equally well have referred to "types of music used in Christian liturgies."

A Definition Broadening Our Horizons

All this necessarily leads to a very considerable expansion of our definition of "ritual music," since it includes all aural practices—vocal or instrumental—integrated in celebration, and moves toward two other areas as well: that of the spoken voice, and that of ordinary sounds and noises. Without by any means abandoning the most usual practices of our western liturgies, this definition allows us to include anything from the cantillated proclamation of a text to a few notes on a guitar, from the sound of a gong to that of an electronic instrument; nor is this definition limited to what was traditionally referred to as a "chant" or an "organ piece."

Consequently, this type of definition allows us to expand the area of ritual music to areas of sound which in certain cultures do not necessarily belong to what we customarily call "singing" or "music." Below, we will examine the important consequences of such an expansion—above all the richness it brings to the whole area of symbol in liturgy.

2

Christian Ritual Music
in Different Cultures

MUSIC MADE INCARNATE

Christ became incarnate. He became part of a race. He adopted the language, the mode of expression and the attitudes, the dress and customs of his people. Although, like every human being, he was placed in a particular time in history and in a particular country, the message he leaves us is universal in scope, valid for all times and for all regions of the world.

Along with its founder, the church was born into a specific people at a given moment in history. At several stages in its development the church took root in particular cultures (GL 10, p. 122). Far from being a weakness, the diversity that this rooting-process gives birth to is a source of richness, and we can see in it a sign of that incarnation of Christ which never ceases to make itself real in every church and in every historical epoch.

The problem is especially important when it comes to singing and instrumental music since, in order that the faithful can find in music a means for expressing their faith, their petitions, their praise, and their unity, they need a "sonic language" that is in harmony with their culture.

PARTICULAR REPERTOIRES, OFFICIAL REPERTOIRES

This has necessarily resulted in an extreme diversity of styles and forms throughout the centuries and in the various regions of the world. What happens is that the creative dynamism of local churches engenders modes of expression adapted to the needs of these churches. And while doing this, they offer to other churches concrete examples from which these other churches may draw inspiration or which they may even adopt for themselves. In this way liturgical repertoires are gradually born, varying in how widespread they are, how lasting they are, how far they are adaptable to the sensitivities they are meant to serve.

All this certainly constitutes a richness, but it also represents a danger. Missionary enthusiasm is constantly confronted with this risk because, without even being aware of it, the bearers of the message come with their cultural baggage, the memories of their most intense spiritual experiences, and therefore often with the desire to communicate to others the very forms wherein they have lived out those experiences. This means that they practice a sort of cultural exportation process whose results are ambiguous. In a country that is rich in a different culture, they cannot always see the limitations of their own culture. They bring the message, but perhaps forget not only that they too have something to receive from this land that makes them so welcome but also that they should be trying to integrate themselves as much as possible into this new culture.

Linked to this phenomenon is a search for the unity desired by Christ himself. The desire to translate this into a visible reality has given rise over the centuries to many different forms of centralization. This tendency, though understandable, carries with it a double danger for liturgy: centralization either results in forms that are neutral and in a way of celebrating that is disincarnate, or else centralization imposes on all the churches a type of celebration belonging to whichever church is chosen as the model. In both cases uniformity pays a considerable price, since it does not normally allow complete involvement of the person, not to mention all that person's cultural potential. Proceeding in this way runs the risk of leading to a deep-frozen liturgy, regulated by exterior discipline, more concerned with respect for forms than with the authenticity of what is done.

Above all, it has been the Roman Church which has manifested this concern for centralization (GL 26, p. 134), channeling all forces toward a central point and governing everything from Rome. This is the source of the dream of a unified liturgy for the whole world, with a single language—Latin (GL 24, p. 132)—and a single musical repertoire—Gregorian chant.

Within the missionary effort that has developed over the past century, we have been more sensitive to the needs of peoples than to their own resources. People of every race and culture were waiting to hear the Good News: we would therefore bring it to them in its Roman wrapping. We are already able to stand back from history far enough to judge that this had a certain value, a certain generosity, and a certain richness, but also certain limits and risks.

If we believed in the universality of the musical language of Gregorian chant, there were in fact some good reasons for it. For example, the exceptional cohesion of melody with text, the relative ease of execution, and above all the exceptional interiorization of expression—all this allowed the widest range of peoples to appreciate the value of this form of music. An additional factor was probably the far-off and anonymous origins of this art: in the cultural domain, the ancient provenance of a work very often reinforces respect and admiration. These different reasons gave rise to the primacy accorded Gregorian chant in the Roman Church during the time when Latin was the sole liturgical language.

In smaller cultural areas which nevertheless made use of a single language we find an analogous phenomenon—e.g., the Lutheran chorale or the Huguenot psalter which constituted the base on which the traditional repertoires of certain Reformed Churches were constructed (GL 43, p. 153).

Regardless of the circumstances marking the development of music in the Christian Churches, regardless of the historical facts, we must acknowledge that the Gospel delivers no "technical notes" telling composers what pathways to follow ... Today's musicians feel that if they are invited to write for the liturgy then it is first of all in their own language and in their own style.

THE TRUE SPECIFICITY OF CHRISTIAN RITUAL MUSIC

The specific nature of Christian ritual music is not found in the realms of form, style, or language, but rather in the manner in which a particular kind of music is integrated into the liturgy. The mere fact that it is culturally adapted to a liturgical assembly is not sufficient to make it automatically a type of ritual music valid for that community. The fundamental condition is as follows: is it possible to make of this music an organic element in the overall liturgical action? Of necessity there is a relationship between music and one of the other essential components (made up of words and actions) of the celebration: the memorial of the death and resurrection of Christ, the actual announcing of his message, and the waiting for the coming of the Kingdom, and thus the conversion of believers, their petitioning, and the constant re-animation of that faith through the power of grace acting in them, and their thanksgiving and praise for the wonders already done for them. No musical act can be alien to any one of the components of liturgy, and the possibility of using a chant or an instrumental piece in a celebration will depend on how easily it can be integrated into the whole (GL 5, p. 118).

The coming Kingdom is being built in each and every effort of individuals and communities to live out the demands of that Kingdom. The "kingdom which is not of this world" (Jn 18:36) must begin to become real in each of our daily lives. And so there is nothing astonishing in saying that Christian ritual music should be intimately linked to the culture in which that liturgy is made incarnate.

Two Characteristics

All Christian liturgy is constructed as a function of two axes:

1. The first axis is constituted in the assembly of the faithful; and therefore, as we will see in Chapters 3 and 4, the music used in liturgy always has a relationship with the people who make up the assembly, whether they perform this music themselves or are associated with it in a different way.

2. The second axis is found in the word of God, on which all Christian celebration is founded—hence the essential importance of the proclamation of texts from Scripture and the response of the assembly; hence, too, the primacy of place given to the singing that carries the words. We will further develop this second aspect in Chapter 5.

Music Apt for Its Purpose

To say that there is no music specifically for Christian liturgy is not to say that Christian liturgy uses any kind of music with indifference. Liturgy necessarily selects from within ancient repertoire or contemporary creations those pieces that can be organically integrated into the ensemble of the liturgical action.

If necessary, the liturgy carries out certain adjustments called for by this integration. Ritual music, a precious element in celebration, is not an end in itself in the same way as (for most performers and listeners) music at a concert is.

The liturgy is led, therefore, to choose and to remove from the celebration certain forms which may be completely valid in themselves but which are ill-suited to this particular usage. (For example, it is now impossible to have a polyphonic *Sanctus* sung by the choir alone if we take seriously the invitation extended to the whole assembly at the end of the preface.) On the other hand, the liturgy sometimes gives birth to a need to revive or restore ancient forms which researchers discover in their own cultural past or in the history of other peoples.

CHOICES TO BE MADE

Many reasons can compel us to remove certain pieces from liturgical usage. For example, a chant constructed on a theme from a well-known symphony or a current pop song embodies in itself such a weight of connotations that it is impossible to detach it from its original form and function, and above all from the cultural symbol that it has become. This sort of thing can happen in different cases: deliberate adaptation, unconscious reminiscence, accidental effect. The most difficult incompatibilities arise with the themes of chants or songs, since it is practically impossible to expunge from one's memory a text that has already been implanted there by the music.

But the same problem can arise with pieces that evoke no precise memories at all. There can be a real problem regarding a piece's liturgical usefulness if the style of the piece, its instrumentation, or its manner of performance recall areas of life judged incompatible with the celebration.

This is perhaps equally true of music of religious inspiration, and even of music created for liturgical use, if the piece carries with it the imprint of a cultural ambience that is too far removed from what we expect of liturgy. Most Masses written in the eighteenth and nineteenth centuries, even if they were conceived in accordance with the liturgical norms current at the time, now appear too theatrical or expressionistic for our sensibilities today. Written for

Notre Dame in Paris, an organum (GL 36, p. 146) by Perotin would be difficult to incorporate into a liturgy of the word at Notre Dame today because of the work's excessive length and the manner in which the text is treated.

An analogous gulf can sometimes be seen with contemporary repertoires. An assembly accustomed to using chorales or psalm-tones would have some difficulty in adopting chants in a very different style without prior preparation—e.g., pieces rich in long melismata or melodies close to contemporary pop songs—even if these chants were conceived for liturgical use and work well in other communities.

NEW PATHWAYS AND REDISCOVERIES

If we are led to make choices and to reject (for various reasons) certain pieces belonging to the surrounding culture but judged to be incompatible with the demands of the liturgy, the opposite phenomenon can also occur. Indeed, it can happen that certain works coming from a completely different culture can be adapted to the liturgy. By taking them over, we contribute to an enrichment of the repertoire and at the same time we open up new cultural horizons.

The question here is one of particular practices and forms. For instance, certain types of responsorial singing or dialogued melodies, so very useful for liturgy, will probably return to use because of the recent craze for certain very ancient forms of popular song based on the repetition of short formulas, even though, for all intents and purposes, these particular musical genres disappeared from our repertoires with the development of musical notation and the abandonment of purely oral tradition (GL 34, p. 143).

A whole threshold here is opening up for researchers and musicologists; it is also a pathway for composers who may feel that these rediscoveries are inviting them to create new ways in which these old forms can function today.

A COMPLEX UNIVERSE

These choices and creative researches cannot, however, be realized in a purely musical context. Singing and instrumental music are indeed constantly linked with the whole canvas over which they are deployed.

The celebration itself is a totality, integrating very diverse elements in the most organic way possible: a place, its décor, its space; texts, chants, instrumental music; movements, postures, human gestures. The interpersonal relationships that are deployed on such a canvas can range from a hieratic frigidity to a fraternal warmth. All these factors have interplay one with another. The music itself, like all the other components of this vast symbolic ensemble, is both a giver and a receiver. It profoundly influences atmosphere and expression; in return, the exterior context, the general ambience, and especially the quality of human relationships within the group can considerably modify our perception of the music.

In short, we have been talking about the complexity of all the problems in which liturgy meets the most imponderable aspects of culture.

3

Singers and Musicians

PEOPLE WHO CELEBRATE

In the past much was written about rites, liturgical objects and vestments, the architecture of churches and their interior décor, musical repertoires and instruments. We have been very preoccupied with forms and materials, and yet we have often neglected to speak about the most essential element: the people who celebrate the liturgy. It is certainly easier to comment on and regulate these exterior aspects than it is to deepen what is going on in the hearts of men and women taking part in a celebration.

And yet we know only too well that buildings, artifacts, and musical scores are dead if no one inhabits them, or animates them, or gives them life. Since the God of Jesus Christ must be adored "in spirit and in truth" (Jn 4:23), it is truly in the hearts of people that we find the source of prayer, whether it is personal prayer or communal prayer.

When studying a liturgical problem, or preparing a celebration, or presiding, or animating, it is with respect to people that we must judge and anticipate and act. When we participate in liturgy, whether as a simple member of the assembly or with a function to perform, we should always feel ourselves to be involved as conscious and free human beings, and not like plain cogs enmeshed willy-nilly in the running of a machine.

PEOPLE GATHERED IN ASSEMBLY

The liturgy, "the summit towards which the activity of the Church is directed" (Constitution on the Sacred Liturgy, no. 10) cannot be conceived of without an assembly, since the very word *ecclesia*, church, means "assembly." Everything taking place in the course of a celebration concerns everyone who takes part in it.

This might seem self-evident, but we need to remind ourselves of it because the Roman Church slipped into certain practices that were difficult to reconcile with this fundamental rule: the monastic habit of celebrating several individual Masses simultaneously; the recitation of the breviary or the rosary during the eucharist; the assembly's responses confined to an altar server or given by the priest himself; the communal singing of the *Sanctus* reserved for choir alone; Masses that became excuses for hearing continual concert-playing by prestigious organists—so many countersigns evidencing a weakening of the sense of the assembly.

This progressive disappearance of the assembly's active participation resulted in a situation which can be summarized as follows:

• the priest said and did everything, and even to the extent of responding to himself;
• when there was dialogue, anything normally belonging to the assembly was taken over by its representatives, namely, by the servers or choir members.

Even if the priest had formulated all his prayers in the plural, it would have been difficult, fifty years ago, to imagine giving him the title of "presider over the assembly"—a description traditionally used in Christian antiquity (GL 39, p. 149).

In the sixteenth century Luther and Calvin were very insistent on the active role of the assembly, notably by means of communal singing (GL 4, p. 117). In the Roman Church we had to wait for the twentieth-century liturgical renewal and Vatican II in order to see a sense of the assembly (GL 3, p. 115) made a visible reality in the rites and therefore in the chants of the rites. The theological rediscovery of the assembly's central role and the concrete efforts aimed at bringing about its active participation—vernacular texts, a style of singing within the grasp of inexpert performers, layout of churches more conducive to good relationships, reordering of the space in older buildings, development of sound systems, proliferation of books and sheets to enable the involvement of the faithful in prayers and singing—all bear witness to an immense twentieth-century enterprise whose purpose is to restore to the assembly the primordial role which rightfully belongs to it. We are today more aware of the ideal toward which we are to strive, and yet the results are often far removed from this ideal. Some celebrations are full of life, and yet how many more are tedious, empty, and anonymous.

There are two main reasons for this.

1. The theology of the assembly has remained very theoretical; it has not been absorbed by Christian communities, some of whose members still live according to the norms of "attending" an obligatory Mass or according to the habits of an interior and individualistic participation in rites that others accomplish in their name. Concrete efforts are often limited to merely technical and exterior aspects. The sense of the assembly has not become a deep-seated conviction, a way of life.

2. The bursting-asunder of modern society has broken down a whole series of social links and family relationships, destroying the spirit of the parish or the locality. A massive over-emphasis on material well-being has generated an obsession with personal comfort, and therefore with the acquisition and spending of wealth. All this operates to the detriment of human relationships and to an authentic sense of festivity. Artificially, we wanted to re-create "loving and festive assemblies" at the very moment when traditional communities were dissolving.

Doubtlessly we will have to wait before the Gospel's message of love and communion becomes for all Christians a really vital need: perhaps then we will finally discover, from the depths of our loneliness, how to aspire to form real communities whose weekly meeting in the presence of the Lord can really be called "assemblies." Only then will the faithful, gathered in their churches, again know how to sing "with a single voice" (Rm 15:6).

This does not necessarily mean that everything will be sung by everyone. Just as the presiding celebrant exercises a particular function and carries out certain actions, so the psalmist, for example, sings a psalm text by herself or himself. The cantor or the choir performs those verses of a song that are too difficult for the assembly.

In each of these cases, what is done by a minister or by a group is lived out in respect of everyone present and is addressed to everyone. It is, therefore, always a "communal action." In this way the assembly's participation in singing and other liturgical actions can assume a number of forms: the more the assembly carries out these actions by itself, the more it is associated with them through an attentive participation. Such diversity enables the avoidance of the dangers of exhaustion and levelling-out. It gives the whole celebration a varied profile, rich in meaning, and with a beneficial sense of variety.

Whether we are talking about an already lengthy tradition, as in the Reformed Churches, or a recent rediscovery, as in the Roman Church, the singing of the Christian assembly must be the object of special care since, in order to be truly lived out, this participation must be compatible with the sensitivity and social customs of the group in question. A constant watchfulness and an unceasing questioning are indispensable, for ritualism and routine can threaten the most life-filled tradition.

THE DISTRIBUTION OF THE ASSEMBLY'S MUSICAL TASKS

When we study the structuring of liturgical assemblies, and especially the division of musical roles within the Roman Church, it is surprising how many different concepts are revealed by history (GL 31, p. 140). We are even more astonished that the regulations in force thirty years ago gave us the image of a hieratic and uniform liturgy, a liturgy little influenced by the cultures in which it took flesh.

During previous periods the manner of celebrating certainly reflected much more of the surrounding concept of hierarchy and life in society, which gave rise to quite diverse solutions. But other factors were also responsible for influencing the division of roles within the assembly.

Influence of Political Models

Relationships between people forming the celebrating community are often affected by the socio-political context—even negatively, by resisting a new trend in the name of tradition. In a society where hierarchical degrees are very visible—for instance, an imperial or monarchic or feudal or military regime—the accentuation of sharing out of roles is perceived as a normal element: the place of the presider over the assembly is then emphasized, and the animator will tend to become very directive. On the other hand, a very democratized political system—an egalitarian conception of society, social customs rich in popular meeting-points—will favor collective and spontaneous forms of expression: communal singing, processions, postures that show the personality of the various "actors." In a well-conceived liturgy, these two values should not be opposed but rather work together. Even if the liturgy inevitably is subject to the influences of the surrounding milieu, it cannot abandon the signs of what is in fact its essence; and the liturgy must also be a sign not only of the Covenant offered by God to believers (through the liturgy's hierarchical structure and dialogued forms) but also a sign of the communion of Christians united in a single faith (through communal prayer and singing).

Influence of Social Usages

Even more than the political context, the cultural customs of each race profoundly influence liturgical practice. Thus it is that societies where tribal traditions remain very much alive will much more spontaneously practice collective singing than societies whose members, even when concentrated in high-density built-up areas, jealously seek to preserve their individuality and their private life. In some countries, a woman acting as a reader or as a solo singer can cause astonishment, whereas such reserve has totally disappeared in other regions.

Influence of Technical Evolution

A relatively strong voice is needed if a person is to speak in church or sing a solo. The appearance, the invasion of sound systems even in small chapels now allows an adequate projection of any kind of voice, and this has tended to promote the use of soloists.

On the other hand, our ears are so used to hearing the sound of voices projected by loudspeakers that we almost blot out the effect of distance and anonymity which indirect transmission produces. Indeed the opposite is the case, for by singing or speaking very close to the microphone you can now create an atmosphere of intimacy and contact that was formerly impossible and which can sometimes even appear suspect.

Reflecting Current Cultural Musical Practices

In such cases the liturgy evolves technically and at the same time comes close to the forms of communication practiced in the world of entertainment. Thus soloists are much more easily accepted in liturgy in proportion as solo stars have developed in the area of pop music, profiting from the advances brought about by technology. In the same way, the styles and forms of communication used in liturgy have been subject to the influence of what is seen in the theater and on television: style of singing, performance by soloists or by groups, type of accompaniment.

Singing by the assembly will probably progress more rapidly when a number of pop singers acquire the habit of regularly involving their listeners in singing with them (see GL 50, p. 164).

Musical Resources

Some composers are good at seeing what singing by an assembly can really be like, and so they willingly write for the assembly. Others feel more at home in composing works destined for choirs. Still others know how to bring to life organic dialogues between soloists, choir, and assembly. The diffusion of a particular type of repertoire automatically contributes to the corresponding form in the structuring of assemblies.

The presence of a soloist or an instrumentalist in a parish also favors choosing a repertoire that is suited to these human resources, and this will gradually model the customs of the community without necessitating a basic choice of principle.

Influence of the Theology of the Assembly

All liturgy presupposes a God and human beings. A large number of practical consequences depend on how the relationship between these two poles is conceived. Opposing a "liturgy for God" to a "liturgy for human beings" constitutes an explicative vision that is both simplistic and dangerous, but which nevertheless allows certain options to be understood.

If there is a preoccupation with worship to be rendered to God, priority will be given to everything that favors this particular dimension: "stretched out" architecture; very high churches; remote and hidden altars, or at least altars very clearly separated from their naves; multiplication of screens, curtains, and grilles; ministers turning their backs to the people; minimal or even non-existent interpersonal relationships. In this context, an unreal, ethereal kind of music is naturally preferred, and it is desirable that the sound source be remote and invisible (choir loft, nuns' choir); the text may not be understandable (Latin phrases lost in the midst of vocalises or polyphony), but the actual meaning of the text is less important and in this way the image of a majestic, remote, and inaccessible God is projected.

On the contrary, if one's first thought is of the assembly, if theology sensitizes Christians to the presence of God in the midst of God's gathered people and to the fact that God comes among us, then the results will certainly be very different, and in several different areas: churches centered around the altar, a circular or triangular design, the presiding celebrant turned toward the assembly and looking at the gathered people in order to speak to them in their own tongue and to enable them to see ritual gestures; insistence on relationships within the group (welcoming, rite of peace, sharing the Gospel, intentions for prayer which recall the problems of the world and those of the local community). And quite naturally this conception of liturgy will use dialogue forms, communal singing, unison music, and unanimous acclamation.

We should, therefore, not be scandalized by the changes that history or experience show us; rather, we should try to understand the values involved in each situation, drawing inspiration from them in order to achieve the best possible balance, and recognizing in this very diversity a sign of the extraordinary richness that exists in the world of liturgy.

In reacting against the excesses inherited from previous centuries, Vatican II has resolutely turned us toward the second option. This theological concept of a God present in his people is properly Christian, whereas the first image—the remote God—can be found in any religion.

MINISTRIES

This human level of structures and roles, however, takes on further significance in the eyes of faith. Indeed, internal hierarchy, relationships of a social nature, and all the activities within the assembly assume a symbolic meaning: they are signs of the life-giving presence of the Spirit.

Singing by the whole assembly manifests the action of the Spirit in each one of its members, animating them, setting them alight, and allowing them access to that communal and fraternal dimension which is proper to the church and leads to a point where individual preoccupations are left far behind.

And again, when a soloist sings—whether this person is the presiding celebrant, an expert or inexpert soloist, or a simple member of the faithful (GL 49, p. 163)—the soloist's contribution is a translation of the diversity of the action of the Spirit, distributing different gifts to each one in order that they should fulfill one role or another in the community. It is certain that the actual reality too often obscures how these contributions are perceived—especially if the attitude of an "actor" or a soloist is only too reminiscent of a pop star in a show, or if an only-too-visible incompetence or a flagrant lack of preparation become countersigns.

Over the centuries the church has adopted different solutions to define the status of its ministers. Priests and deacons are ordained ministers who commit themselves definitively to the service of the church. The office of reader was once (GL 42, p. 152) an instituted ministry, and it was the same, for a period, for the psalmist (GL 40, p. 150). Today these functions are generally considered as occasional services, requested of those members of the assembly who are capable of carrying them out in a competent manner.

Whether or not it is a case of an instituted or ordained ministry, the various liturgical functions need to be lived out as services rendered and as living signs of the Holy Spirit's action in the church.

Thus the very functioning of the liturgy determines a certain number of roles:

• the whole assembly, as the People of God, confesses its faith, joins in petition and thanksgiving, and thus manifests its unity and its ecclesial dimension;

• the ministers (presider, deacon, reader . . .) fulfill various functions, especially in the context of the unfolding of the celebration (greetings, invitations, monitions), the proclamation of the word (psalmist), and of animation;

• the director of ministries of music in the United States serves in both a volunteer and a paid position, some full-time and many part-time; this person serves as the overall coordinator of musical activities and musical-liturgical education in the parish;

• the groups of cantors, whether a small nucleus of people who sing the verses or a larger schola or even a large choir, sing for the assembly or with the assembly, depending on the nature of the chants and their place in the celebration;

• instrumentalists (organists or others) introduce, accompany, or prolong the chants of the ministers, of the groups of cantors, and especially those of the assembly; they create sonic spaces designed to indicate the feast or to promote meditation;

• composers and those who organize liturgies, even if their role is not exercised within the assembly, must in some way anticipate the experience of the celebration if their work is to allow the Christian people to find the language of its prayer at the appropriate moment.

This simple listing suffices to show the great diversity of musical roles necessary for the liturgy.

Singing by the Assembly and Other Musical Functions

We should note that the most essential of all these functions is not that of specialist musicians, however important their function may be. What is most essential is singing by the assembly since the assembly's function is to manifest the very essence of the celebrating community and its unity brought about by the action of the Holy Spirit.

The first Christian communities understood this very well, and singing by the assembly is mentioned from apostolic times onwards both in historical documentation and in normative texts (GL 51, p. 164).

The church at the end of the twentieth century occasionally has some difficulty in rediscovering this type of singing, whose value has been gradually eroded over the centuries. In certain regions the church even went so far as to abolish all sung elements. In most cases, the church contented itself with singing by the ministers and by the choir. But we should also note that the rediscovery of singing by the assembly does not entail a lessening of musical responsibilities on the part of soloists or specialized groups: on the contrary, it gives them value and allocates them their proper place, by allowing a more precise definition which leads to a discovery of their true meaning.

4

Music for Everyone

MUSIC, SYMBOLIC SIGN AND RITE

Liturgy is a symbolic action. It includes a considerable number of symbols (GL 54, p. 167) of a visual or aural nature. The words used are charged for the believer with an inexhaustible and ever-fertile richness of meaning. Exterior gestures and postures always signify interior attitudes. The structure of the celebrating group symbolizes a type of relationship that goes beyond the members constituting the group. Liturgical vestments, images, locations, and signs of all kinds refer us to things other than themselves.

If the role of music is not limited to being simply decoration, if music really becomes one of the components of liturgy, then music is necessarily involved in this symbolic nature. By integrating itself in the sacramental order, music is the bearer of more than just music itself, and thus it becomes the way the members of the assembly express themselves.

In particular, the function (GL 15, p. 125) of communal singing is to signify communion in unity for the assembly—a communion desired by the Lord who calls together the assembly. The dialogue between the presider and the members of the assembly symbol-izes the Covenant between God and humanity. Unison singing, better than any other form, is able to translate unanimity (GL 58, p. 170) of spirit, whereas polyphony can become an image of the plurality of particular callings and of the unity sought by the harmonization of different gifts. Styles, contrasting nuances, the opposing poles of times of silence and moments of outburst of sound—the most varied musical elements can become bearers of meaning. They recount the death and resurrection of Christ; they translate the weakness and the hope of the sinner; they announce the Kingdom of God that is built when Christians really allow themselves to be reborn—a new humanity, fertilized by participation in the mystery of a Christ dead and risen: a mystery lived out in the innermost depths of their hearts.

In order to become a symbolic sign, music, like other ritual elements, is integrated into the totality of the liturgical action. Music becomes a rite in itself, a rite accomplished in the very bosom of the assembly, for the assembly and, often, by the assembly. But such a role has its demands. It presupposes in particular that the dialogues are real exchanges, that unison singing brings together all available voices into a real unison, that the harmony of the choir is in tune and correctly balanced. It also presupposes that the music offered to the faithful is suited to their abilities, when they are to sing, and to their perceptive faculties, when they are to listen.

We should remember that the "active participation" demanded by the council does not mean that the assembly must itself carry out all the actions and sing all the chants in the liturgy. In certain cases, the assembly will be actively involved in the performance of a rite; in others, the assembly is united by a global participation in the rite that is being accomplished by certain "actors," ministers, soloists, choirs, or instrumentalists (GL 1, p. 113).

SINGING BY THE ASSEMBLY

When it is the role of the assembly to sing a chant, it is obviously useful for that particular piece to be within its grasp. This does not meaning confusing ease of use with banality. But there exist, in popular music as in the works of the great masters, marvelous melodies of wonderful simplicity. It would be unjust to have an *a priori* mistrust of singing by the assembly on the pretext that such singing can never attain a high technical level. Even with simple forms, singing by the assembly can attain a high expressive quality. Everyone can recall examples of celebrations that were striking by the vigor, the conviction, and the warmth of what was sung (GL 50, p. 164).

In practical terms, the style of pieces destined for an assembly must correspond to the musical language used by the surrounding society—music that is simple to perform but at the same time easy to "understand" and to accept.

Certain rules, according to countries, can be formulated as to the limits of the vocal range to be used (in English-speaking countries we tend to use the limits of low C to high D), the rhythms that are possible (for example, French-speaking assemblies tend to iron out syncopations), the intervals that are singable (chromatic movement, augmented fourths, leaps of a seventh are only possible in certain contexts which facilitate their performance).

Analogous rules can be found for the writing of texts since full participation cannot be achieved if the members of the assembly are unable to find the language of their prayer in the texts that are sung.

SINGING AND INSTRUMENTAL MUSIC PERFORMED
ON BEHALF OF THE ASSEMBLY

There is more room for maneuver when it comes to musical elements whose performance does not depend on the capabilities of the assembly. Whether it concerns something sung or something played, performers will want to prepare these pieces. As for the listeners, they will often accept strange or difficult music when they do not have to perform it themselves. Just as it is easier to understand a language than actually to speak it, so it is easier to accept music that is listened to rather than music that is to be performed.

The liturgy includes numerous occasions when music is performed by people who are to a greater or lesser degree musical specialists:

• elements (lines or verses) of an assembly piece sung by a soloist or by the choir;

• pieces, whether polyphonic or not, performed by the choir alone;

• instrumental pieces that presuppose an accomplished musician.

For the performers the rule is simple: they must only perform pieces that are within their grasp so as to ensure that the work's integrity and style will be respected. For the listening assembly, the possible level is more difficult to determine, since it depends

• on the function of each musical element in the overall celebration, and

• on how well the assembly is prepared, and what it is accustomed to hearing.

When what is sung consists of a text offered to aid meditation—for example a psalm—it is important that text, melody, and style of performance correspond to what the assembly can absorb without arousing rejection. In other cases—during the performance of a polyphonic motet, for example—the text is secondary, and only the music has to have a style that is, if not familiar, at least acceptable to the listeners. On the other hand, tolerance increases when attention is seized by an action and listening becomes less "direct"; but a certain prudence is always necessary. In particular, when an instrumental accompaniment is supporting a text that is read or sung, the "dosage" of such support needs to be carefully monitored. If the music becomes distracting so that the text is not so easily heard, then the music is operating counter to the desired goal.

This is another way of emphasizing the extreme care with which all musical contributions need to be prepared. They presuppose an acute liturgical sensibility and are often limited by relatively harsh constraints, since they have to correspond to the needs of liturgical functionality, and to what the faithful will welcome and pay attention to.

Music Creating a Gulf

We must immediately add that musicians—be they composers, improvisers, performers—have at their disposal a proportionate amount of room for maneuver which they should use with restraint and with a precise awareness of what they are trying to achieve and what is in fact possible.

In fact, regarding what we have just been saying about a conformity between what the assembly can do and the music that is offered to it, a work whose effect is one of surprise can sometimes be beneficial.

Old habits, conformity, routine—all are a constant threat to the liturgy. The same rites, the same words, the same chants coming back time and time again—all these run the risk of weakening the impact of the gospel message. A new type of music, a sonically surprising element, or an unusual style can astonish, challenge, and become a sign of that continual newness of the Gospel, a sign of an interior renewal that every believer should be looking for in every eucharist, a sign of that painful "bringing to birth" from which will issue "the new heavens and the new earth" that we are waiting for (Is 65:17; 66:22; Rom 8:11; 2 Pt 3:13; Rv 21:1).

One of the components of festivity (GL 12, p. 123) has always been this injection of novelty, of the exceptional, of the unheard-of; and this is precisely why festivity needs to be used wisely. Only rarely does "ordinary" liturgy call on this level, which needs to remain exceptional if it is to preserve its value.

What we have here is an opportunity for creative musicians, a call the church addresses to them since they, better than any others, can by their art signify the two complementary values of Christian faith, always constant and ever new. If a really well-known musical language can generate the impression of a familiar world, another language that surprises by its timbre, its inflections, its rhythms, or its harmony can become an eloquent sign of mystery and newness (GL 29, p. 138).

Homogenous Culture and Pluralism

All this is relatively easy in theory since we envision the assembly as a homogenous group more or less in line with our own reactions and our own criteria. This is certainly the case in countries where culture has remained intact and/or where social life presents enough elements of cohesion and stability. In European countries we still find this situation in some homogenous rural communities whose members have all followed the same cultural evolution and have modeled their musical sensibilities in accordance with the "mold" of local liturgical repertoire.

It is also the case in group celebrations—Masses with young people, celebrations during catechetical meetings, religious communities, prayer groups, etc. Their shared interests—resulting in an agreed-upon sensitivity and a spirituality developed through life in common—favor interior unity.

But in most European and North American countries the potpourri of population produced by vacation and by work, the extreme diversity of repertoires and styles diffused by the mass media (TV and radio, cassettes and records), the multiplicity of social and cultural origins in urban and suburban societies—all have irrevocably transformed our celebrating communities. And this has happened within the space of only a few years.

Faced with an "average assembly," we know that from now on there will be no such thing as "average music," and that the musical experiences of the members of the assembly are affected by the fragmentation of music broadcasts on radio and by the type of material available for home audio use.

One advantage of this new cultural situation is that members of our communities have been compelled to acquire a spirit of tolerance to which they were not previously accustomed. Even older people seem to be open to musical styles unknown to them thirty years ago. But, faced with the choices to be made, even this tolerance does not eliminate the problems. How can those responsible resolve these problems and balance the multiple demands of such a pluralism?

Without doubt assemblies will find their language of prayer not in banal or characterless music, but rather in pieces whose texts and music evoke a call to contemplation or to an inner movement. To produce such effects, the style of this music will often be relatively classical; and yet it will avoid banality if the textual and musical content succeeds in taking hold of the performers and the listeners in their entirety, offering them sufficiently deep elements for meditation, and sufficiently dynamic melodic or rhythmic movements, so that their life forces, both intellectual and emotional, are stimulated. Music that is simple but alive can allow people from completely different backgrounds to encounter each other again in a language that is common to all of them.

This will not prevent the musician or the liturgical organizer from integrating certain elements in different styles, even in strange styles. This type of stylistic pluralism within the totality of a celebration can, if correctly used and even commented on, enrich the whole and become the sign of that renewal which each eucharist should also be achieving.

These difficult demands of our current liturgy offer an opportunity both to composer and to assembly; they help the members of the assembly celebrate in truth, respecting mutual differences, recognizing in these differences that divine richness which is always greater than ourselves.

5

Word and Singing

The faculty for wonderment and for expressing this feeling seems to be inscribed in human nature. Praise forms the primary language of all conscious creatures who discover the mystery of their own existence and the richness of the world around them.

In Genesis (2:19-20), the man is invited by God to give names to the beings that surround him. In learning to see and recognize these beings in order to name them, in learning to give thanks to the Lord for the wonders that the Lord creates without ceasing, human beings acquired that "wisdom" (GL 22, p. 130), that art of conscious living which determines their rightful position and their role of interpreter of the unconscious universe before its Creator. Thus one of the first things that humanity was called to do was to give praise. And praise becomes explicit with Christian revelation. Speaking of Christ (Eph 1:11-12), St. Paul affirms that "we were predestined to be the praise of his glory."

If God created us as capable of wonder and praise, it is because this praise constitutes the necessary and irreplaceable response to the Creator's act, freely given. If God awaits this praise from us, it is because such praise allows us to be fully living: it allows us to become aware of the marvels that God accomplishes in the material and human universe which surrounds us and, if we wish, the marvels which God accomplishes within us through the divine grace which produces a new humanity according to the Gospel. In proclaiming the wonders of God, we become God's "partners and interpreters."

We need praise so that we might get outside ourselves, open ourselves to the world and to others, expand ourselves, and thus gradually get close to our real dimension.

This slow human growth, far from centering us on our own image through an egotistical turning back in on ourselves, actually leads us to enter into an intimate contact with other human beings. The act of praise, here again, can help us to vibrate with the rhythm of the life everywhere around us, to tune us into the vital rhythm of our human brothers and sisters.

But the simple words of our language are not enough to provide us with the totality of that experience, for they run the risk of interning us within a sort of scientific, notional inventory which is incapable of showing forth the emotion which accompanies our discovery. In order to show forth that emotion, praise turns itself into poetry, words and phrases digging deep into their rhythms and their sonorities and creating in their action a new form that is somehow mysteriously capable of becoming the "carrier wave" for the globality of this experience (GL 38, p. 148). Going further, poetic language makes music of itself, finally reaching the new entity that we call human singing, at once both text and melody, knowledge and emotion, an evocation of beings and expression of the Being who expresses himself by uttering what he reveals.

This *raison d'être* of singing appears in the Old Testament, and the whole Jewish tradition is one of praise. It continues uninterruptedly into the New Testament, and when Jesus "says the blessing" (Mt 26:26; Mk 14:22), he is entering a secular tradition which he renews from within in order to lead it, without destroying anything, to the full dimension of the eucharist.

Believers of all ages have found within themselves this extraordinary capacity for singing, singing which respects the words but which exalts and lifts them up to new heights of expression, going even further when gesture and dance are also involved. We should therefore find nothing astonishing in the fact that the liturgy has always traditionally accorded such an important place to singing by the community—singing that is based on the word.

COMMUNAL PRAISE

Indeed, solitary wonderment is not enough. We feel deeply within ourselves—at least at certain decisive moments in our existence—the need to communicate, to be in communion with the other members of our human communities, to share and express our praise with them. This communal dimension is itself also engraved into our nature. This is why God, in the New Covenant as in the Old, invites his people to praise him. Each assembly of believers, at the same time both a cell and an image of the church, a people born anew out of the Pentecost event to "proclaim the wonders of God" (Acts 2:11), has as its primary vocation the expression of praise. The eucharist (GL 11, p. 122) and the liturgy of the hours (GL 27, p. 136) continue the praise of the psalms and inscribe themselves into the immense chant of all sentient beings, on earth and everywhere.

In a grandiose vision the Book of Revelation conjures up (chapters 4, 5, 7, 14, 15, 16, 19, 21) the form of worship rendered to the One who sits on the throne and to the Lamb: a form made up of movements and gestures (the immense procession and the postures of the elect), of singing (their acclamations), and of music (the harps of the twenty-four old men and the angelic trumpets). Without a doubt we are supposed to see in this evocation a celestial model of the liturgy to which we are summoned here and now and which will blossom forth in eternity. For, if praise is natural for human beings from their very beginnings, it will constitute the *raison d'être* of the redeemed. Between these two poles, even if many of our contemporaries think that something freely given must therefore necessarily be useless, praise still remains for human communities that indispensable space which opens them up to their future dimension.

In fact, in our earthly liturgy, "we taste of the powers of the world to come" (Heb 6:4,5). We participate, in union of intention and by anticipation, in the heavenly liturgy "with the angels and archangels, and all the powers of heaven" (as the prefaces state it) to sing the acclamation of the thrice-holy God.

SINGING IN A BROAD SENSE

When we speak of singing, we often limit ourselves to a few rather precise forms to which our surrounding culture has accustomed us. But here we should understand "singing" in a more complete sense, encompassing extremely diverse forms of expression.

In reality, there is singing the moment we leave the current state of language by bringing in a new sonic element. We can include in this idea a whole range of forms:

• text recited *recto tono*—i.e., on a single, unvarying note, abandoning the natural inflexions of spoken language. The former *Dominus vobiscum* would be a good example;

• "cantillation", when the text is declaimed with melodic inflections which are not the same as those of ordinary speech nor as those of "melody" with precise and measurable intervals. Black people are wonderful at this form, which we have lost in white culture;

• "psalmodized" text, combining recitative on an unvarying note with a few melodic formulas. Examples of this would be the psalms in the office, and the institution narrative in the eucharist;

• syllabic chant, in which melody is made up of a succession of single notes, each corresponding to a syllable of the text. The religious song, the chorale, and the hymn often belong to this genre;

• ornamented singing in which certain syllables—perhaps all of them—are sung to several notes. Most of the pieces in the Gregorian Graduale made use of this form;

• the vocalise, in which a single syllable is developed with long flights of contemplative or expressive notes. The melismata of the Alleluia in Gregorian chant are the most typical example in the western repertoire.

There are no watertight compartments separating these genres: they can be mixed and combined. Each can have a place in the liturgy, and choosing one or another will depend essentially on the importance that the text should have in each particular case and on the level of expression desired.

DIVERSITY OF VOCAL ACTS AND DIVERSITY OF FORMS

Like life today, the liturgy uses language in multiple ways: to greet, to challenge or acclaim, to communicate a message, to make reply and indicate agreement, to re-state and approve. For all these different vocal acts, the liturgy needs modes of communication that are suitable for each of these functions (GL 23, p. 131):

• the simple transmission of a spoken message (monition, announcement);

• dialogue, made up of an exchange of calls and responses (greetings, invitatories, dismissal);

- prayer, often formulated by a single person and to which the others respond with a brief Amen (prayer) or by a refrain (general intercessions);
- reading, which transmits a message (readings in the liturgy of the word);
- recitative, a sort of melodic canvas designed for the absorption and savoring of a text in the course of meditation (psalmody);
- proclamation and praise, announcing the wonders of God and inviting to thanksgiving (preface);
- cry and acclamation, where a member of the assembly, or a group, or the whole assembly expresses an outburst of joy, of praise or of supplication (Alleluia, "Glory to you, Lord," *Kyrie*);
- unanimous singing, expressing the involvement, thanksgiving, or praise of the assembly (hymns, songs).

The link between the text and the music will vary considerably between these various verbo-musical genres. Basically there are two factors:

1. Genre of the texts used

Texts have different natures. Some are poetic, some not so poetic. Some act as a leaven that gives birth to music, others are not so good at doing this. Certain texts are simple elements of information and cannot stand being sung. The more lyrical a text is, the more chance it has of lending itself to being set to music. A text like the Beatitudes (Mt 5:3-12), for instance, can favor this form of performance because of the use of the same word at the beginning of each phrase (which creates a sort of initial rhyme) and even more because of the binary structure of each unit. A poem, by its very nature, gives an invitation to go beyond the words and often produces an appeal for music. And then there are certain texts, conceived for use as hymns, which suffer when they are spoken rather than sung.

The opposite is true in the case of the dogmatic character of the Nicene Symbol (Creed) which certainly does not call for a musical setting, both by reason of its text and by reason of our own sensibilities.

2. Type of communication set up between the speakers

The nature of the text is, obviously, closely linked to the form of communication envisioned, the text actually being formulated with regard to the role that it will have to play. Communication of a message does not work well in a sung form, which would compromise the transmission of its content and would thus betray its character. When a psalm is read, proclaimed, or sung in the presence of an assembly, the faithful who hear it must be able to grasp its meaning: a really suitable musical form will avoid drawing attention to itself or to the art of the performer and will, on the contrary, permit the assimilation of the poetic text by its form and by the type of interpretation it requires.

The role of a choir poses very different problems, depending on the moment and the meaning of its contribution. When the choir sings alone, it may be that the text ought to be comprehensible for the assembly. In this case, the choir must choose suitable forms— i.e., pieces whose musical phraseology serves the text well without enveloping it in a sonic *décor* that is too overwhelming. Unison singing will often be preferable to polyphony, and the singers will concentrate their efforts on the meaning of the text and its correct articulation. In other cases, the choir's role is aiming more at the creation of a festive ambience, or of a certain atmosphere of sound, rather than at the communication of the message. It is then rather less indispensable that the meaning of the words be perceived; and this allows the introduction into the celebration of pieces in other languages, of rich polyphony, of musical works with generously developed vocalises.

When the assembly itself sings, its purpose is not the communication of a message but the very act of singing, which must be adapted (by means of the form of the piece and the manner of performing it) to the appropriate vocal act for each situation. Meditation brought about by a psalm or a prayer requires a relatively discreet kind of music. The responses in a dialogue that is well composed will follow a melodic and rhythmic schema that promotes good linking-together. An authentic acclamation, getting closer to the cry indicated by the word itself, will allow the faithful to express both that interior outburst and its exteriorization, in line with the very nature of the act. The same is true of a petition designed to elicit in the believer at prayer a call, an aspiration, a sense of waiting. Lastly, a hymn of praise should mobilize all the available forces of singers in an act of singing that lasts long enough to allow the warmth of wonder to be born again within them.

So, depending on the priorities needed, the celebration will favor either the text or the melody, depending on whether it is a question of the transmission of a message, or the assimilation of a text, or the unanimous act of singing, or praise for its own sake. Without there being any precise boundaries, one can follow the increase in the role of the music from one stage to another.

With the spoken word, music as such is absent. In proclamation, the choice of the "tone" of voice and the way of articulating the syllables is already entering into categories in the musical domain. However modest it may be, the tone used for psalmody is melodic, but discreet enough to give a complete sense of the shape of the word that is being meditatively savored.

With "verbo-melodism" (GL 59, p. 171) we reach a median zone where text and music blend in a kind of intimacy, the musical values setting the melodic and rhythmic internal values of the text into relief.

From this level onwards, melody becomes more and more important, to the point where it exists by itself. In a chorale, comprehension of the text remains basic, but the melody already constitutes a musical entity by itself. In an aria, the melodic aspect is even more developed, carrying the text a long way from spoken language. Lastly, a vocalise stretches out syllables into long musical phrases which sometimes allow one to forget the word to which they belong (GL 56, p. 168).

The more important the word is, the more music becomes a servant; and, according to how far functions other than simple communication are involved, the word progressively abandons its priority to give more room for musical values.

BEYOND THE MESSAGE

As we saw above, the transmission of God's word and the process of listening to that word are fundamental to all Christian liturgy. Anything to do with the word, therefore, has priority. In order that its message continue to be transmitted, it is necessary that the word be constantly re-spoken, listened to, explained, and assimilated in the church. However, this priority does not destroy all the other functions of language—functions which impinge on the liturgy in many different ways.

• *Sign of unity*

When the whole assembly is invited to sing, whatever the text may be, the assembly's song becomes a sign of its unity through the very fact of singing the same syllables at the same pitch and at the same moment, with no one listening but everyone making an effort to express themselves in communion with the others. While listening to oneself singing, everyone hears each other singing, and this can become the moment when an intense community experience takes place.

• *Unanimity and dialogue*

The community is also a place where exchanges take place. Whatever the intellectual content of the phrases may happen to be, the simple fact of being in dialogue establishes a contact between the participants and becomes a sign of the relationship between them; it also becomes a sign.

• *Sign of differentiation*

We say that we want the liturgy to be integrated into the life of the faithful, but by its very nature the liturgy also constitutes a "time apart" in their lives. The act of singing—because it is gift, because it lasts for a certain time, and because of the way it differs from the spoken word—shows up this necessary differentiation. Rather more so now than formerly, the use of living languages in singing allows us in certain cases to go easily beyond the banality of ordinary conversation and reading aloud.

• *Involvement of the whole person*

Above all, it is when going beyond the realm of ideas that music plays its part—in particular when music allows us to touch the depths of our being, deep in our hearts (GL 18, p. 128), inviting us to welcome the presence of God and of other people, beyond any abstract theory. By the power it has over our sensitivities, music can help us to make this transition from the cerebral to the affective, since our intuitive and affective functions are often misunderstood or devalued by the warped usages of our present civilization.

• *Spontaneous creativity*

One can also imagine the case evoked by Paul (1 Cor 14:26) of a member of the assembly feeling the coming-to-birth within him-

or herself of a real need to create praise. This is obviously an exceptional case, and even free and spontaneous praise normally uses elements composed beforehand. Our innate prudence tends to make us feel rather reserved when faced with spontaneous creativity; often, in order to achieve a single marvelous and enriching success we need to risk undergoing a number of experiences of very doubtful value. But this is not sufficient reason to exclude the possibility of authentic inspiration in this area.

SINGING—A UNIQUE ENTITY

Having already referred to the text and the melody—the components of singing—several times over, we now need to recall the link that binds these two elements together.

A chant is not "the addition of music and text" but a new reality, at once both text and music. The elements are separable in the field of analysis, but inseparable in their lived reality. Text and music give life to each other, mutually enriching each other; but, when separated from each other, neither can be described as a chant any longer. (GL 47, p. 162)

When music becomes a chant, music finds its whole weight in the meaning which the words carry within themselves and which they breathe into the music. When words in their turn become a chant, words can attempt to say that which alone they are incapable of expressing; for music sets them free from their current function and allows them, within this new situation which exalts them, to convey much more than their simple meaning can deliver.

Thus is it that singing, an expression of total humanity, can help us to climb right up to the invisible and ineffable realities toward which we feel ourselves called in the very depths of our being.

6

Music and Instruments

The centrality given to God's word in the liturgy results in singing being given pride of place among all the forms of musical art. As we have seen in the preceding chapter, music works in several different ways in the liturgy as "word made music," whether in the proclamation of a scriptural text, or in meditating upon it, or in restating in today's language the ever-new act of thanksgiving of all believers.

However, this legitimate priority given to sung texts does not mean the exclusion of forms of music that are not word-bearing. Traditionally there are a number of types of vocal music where the text is practically lost in favor of the melody. We find this in long Gregorian melismata—especially in the Alleluia, where the letter "a" can hardly still be perceived as belonging to the original word. In polyphony the same phenomenon is accentuated by the interplay of the voices, which hinder the perception of the text: only the performers can grasp its meaning—assuming that they are even thinking about it, that is. In all these cases the text is nevertheless not totally absent since it serves as a point of departure for the vocalise. The same applies in another technique used by many composers: the sustaining of phrases with humming (GL 19, p. 129). More rarely, this kind of sonority can be used for its own sake without it necessarily having to be a sort of sonic backcloth for accompanying singing by a soloist or a group. When this happens, the human voice joins the great family of musical instruments which is the subject of this chapter.

In this field there are innumerable possibilities. Besides pipe organs, all kinds of instruments are presently used in our churches—classical and popular, ancient and modern, strings, wind and percussion. Modern research has also created a whole range of electro-acoustic instruments. In the same way as traditional instruments, they will doubtless have an increasingly important role to play in the liturgy.[1]

In our culture we are also accustomed to listening to recorded music, to the point where our contemporaries are scarcely capable of perceiving the difference between an instrumental piece performed *hic et nunc* and a piece on a record or tape, if it is reproduced with sufficiently good technology to ensure high quality sound.[2] If there is a problem here, it is rather in the domain of the musical act, which always has priority in a celebration.

A SECULAR EXCLUSION

For a very long time musical instruments were excluded from the liturgy, with very rare exceptions such as bells (GL 6, p. 119) which were used to give aural signals and were employed liturgically in this way and not as sources of music as such. The pipe organ was the only musical instrument permitted in the recent legislation of the Roman Church (Liturgy Constitution, no. 120; Instruction on Music in the Sacred Liturgy, no. 62), and it is still considered by some of the faithful as the only instrument worthy of the liturgy. Such an attitude recalls the mistrust with which all other instruments have been viewed by the official

---

1. The reference here is not so much to electronic organs as to the whole world of the synthesizer. The use of MIDI, computers, and synthesizers appears ready to revolutionize our concepts in certain areas of liturgical music in the years to come.

2. In the United States the National Association of Pastoral Musicians Director of Music Ministries Division issued a position statement clarifying the use of electronic instruments in conjunction with a live performance and the use of electronic instruments as substituting for a live musician. Pre-recorded organ and other instrumental accompaniments, while possible and commercially available, seem to be unsuitable for liturgical use.

documents. In the twentieth century, the progressive admittance of stringed and wind instruments has been marked by some hesitation in the Roman texts, which reflects the absence of any certain principles in this whole area.

This mistrust arose for many different reasons, varying according to culture; but the principle motifs always lead us back to the concern for creating an impermeable boundary between "sacred music" and "profane music." The mere fact that an instrument could be used outside church to make people dance during secular festivities was sufficient reason to ban the use of the same instrument inside a church.

Arguments based on another principle also made their appearance here: an instrument, it was said, does not transmit the word, and it is therefore inappropriate for the liturgy. Some would go even further down this pathway, arguing that the human voice alone is "worthy" to sing the Creator's praises, since the voice was the sole musical instrument given by nature to the human race.

The Eastern Churches continue to exclude instruments from the liturgy: according to their tradition, all musical forms must be bearers of the word (GL 37, p. 146).

On the other hand, the Reformed Churches, sometimes after a period of hesitation (GL 35, p. 144), gave an important place to the organ, to support the voices and to alternate with them. Luther also allowed the use of wind instruments to reinforce melody-lines.

Today Protestant Churches often ask organists to prolong their preluding on the word of God, and their meditation-postludes on the same word, thus creating the right kind of climate for the assimilation of that word by the faithful. This custom, we are happy to say, is now spreading into Catholic worship.

In this whole area, like many others, different traditions have adopted widely varying positions, depending on the amount of weight given to one particular set of values or another. Within a single tradition different choices also evolve in respect to the importance given to one particular theological principle as opposed to another. This is particularly true when it is a question of cultural customs.

In western countries the organ, considered hitherto as the archetypal instrument for church music, is nevertheless a feature of concert halls. The other side of the coin is that brass instruments have found a place in church, and the wave of guitars, flutes, and percussion instruments have considerably enriched the orchestral palette of musical performances.

This has been a major contribution in tearing aside the ideological veil which once marked the frontier between liturgical and profane music. In the same way, the barriers prohibiting access into church of any kind of instrument, no matter what, have been broken down. At first barely tolerated, then accepted, instruments are now seen as greatly enriching the liturgy (GL 30, p. 139). We will see a number of reasons for this, and also some limitations.

At the Service of the Text

Cultural evolution has produced the conditions favorable to such a great change of attitude, and this has happened through the vast increase in everyday listening to musical instruments on disc and on radio. With the latest pop music invading their "space" at every moment of the day, most of our contemporaries now feel frustrated if they are deprived of the sound of the orchestras accompanying their favorite soloists. In church, as elsewhere, we took on the custom of supporting practically every chant; and even plainchant scholas, flying in the face of historical truth, allowed organ accompaniment of Gregorian melody.

In many cases, instrumental support is a precious source of enrichment for what is sung. Chord-changes and percussion emphasize the accents of the text and clarify its structure. When an instrument capable of producing sustained sounds—organ, flute, violin, etc.—doubles the melody, this helps the line and the phrasing. Above all, harmony and instrumental color, when well conceived and well carried out, heighten the expressive value of the melody.

This contribution seems to be especially valuable when used for singing by a community, since an ample instrumental support fills out the singing of the assembly and gives courage even to the most timid, and thus obviously helping to strengthen cohesion and unanimity. What happens at a musical level reverberates in a very real way (even if difficult to quantify) at the level of community life.

As well as playing an accompanying role, the organ and other instruments often enter the scene to introduce items, to give the pitch to the choir or the assembly, and also frequently—and very interestingly, although less directly utilitarian—to prolong an item and lead gradually into silence. This specific role has already been discussed: it offers an excellent example of how instrumental music can contribute when it is an integral part of the celebration.

Nevertheless, if instruments can be placed at the service of texts and rites, using them also carries with it some risks. For example, when the proclamation of a psalm is accompanied by a melody on a flute, this instrumental intervention can often distract the attention of the listeners, preventing them from actually listening to the text. An organ played too powerfully can also overwhelm the voices and drown the text it is supposed to be underpinning. Quite apart from the problem of texts, instruments can also present a danger with regard to the rites: a badly-chosen piece—whether in style, or the atmosphere it creates, or the connotations it brings with it—can alter and compromise the perception of the rite. A brilliant piece, normally played as a recessional voluntary, will inevitably disturb a communion rite.

A concern for liturgical unity therefore imposes an essential rule on instrumental playing: respect for the place of those instruments in the overall ensemble, and thus especially respect for the rites and texts.

LITURGICAL FUNCTIONS PROPER TO INSTRUMENTAL MUSIC

This brings us by a natural progression to another specific role of instrumental music in the liturgy.

If we believe that the liturgy should lead the members of a community to go further than a mere preoccupation with daily demands, in order to open them up to the ever-growing mystery of the Kingdom of God; if we recognize that words, limited to the ideas that they translate, do not always take into account the globality and the depths of the universe they evoke; if we admit that there is in human beings an aspiration to go beyond what we know and can express in order to glimpse (through a sort of intuition rather than mystical ecstasy) the world of the realities of faith—then we can discover a "vocation" for instrumental music which cannot be replaced by anything else.

When singing leads the word beyond itself, music can accompany meditation and prayer in this opening-up, an opening-up so often sought and so rarely achieved, and never realized in its fullness. At this point—at the end of a chant, after a reading or meditation—the playing of music becomes a rite in itself; it constitutes a liturgical time that is given a precise function, just like the ringing of bells signals both physically and symbolically the calling of the believers to an ecclesial gathering-together. During such moments the liturgy is not doing anything else: the musical act constitutes a rite in the full meaning of the word.

But in most cases instrumental music is integrated into the rites, offering its specific contribution to the unfolding of a ritual gesture or an action. So, when an instrumental piece accompanies a procession, it imprints a movement, an interior cadence on that procession, and gives a richer meaning to the action of the participants.

Music can also form "bridges of sound" between two moments in a celebration, providing a painless preparation for certain transitions which a liturgy that is often too rich in different elements actually needs in order to ensure its own indispensable unity. An interlude containing a well-thought-out progression of sound can heal the breach between a very interiorized penitential rite and the festive outbursts of the *Gloria* which follows.

From another perspective, every celebratory action takes place in a certain time-span. This time-span is necessary in order to allow the participants to live out each element. Music without text, often more efficacious than singing if well chosen, can give a direction to that time-span, can structure it and ensure that it comes to a happy end. This is especially true of a lengthy communion rite.

Whether it is itself the center of the rite or merely accompanying a rite that is not of itself musical, instrumental music contributes in an exceptionally productive way to the creation of a proper ambience, festive or recollected in turn; and this proper ambience is needed by the assembly in order to live out the celebration and be permeated with the atmosphere of a liturgical feast, or a liturgical time, or a liturgical moment. Music is particularly useful in this context when it is used at the beginning of celebration to create the "sonic space" in which all the other elements will be inscribed, a little like the overture prepares for and introduces the unfolding of an opera.

Some people reproach music for distracting and turning the faithful away from their prayer, inviting them to become listeners.

But who can really analyze or measure what is going on inside each person? Who can judge for certain what are called the "indeterminable functions" (GL 20, p. 129) of this kind of music?

It is certain that, even more with the average non-musical church-goer than with the musician who is always tempted to analyze while listening, music creates within our beings those mysterious movements that are both physical and psychic which can be felt as tangible signs of a leap forward or of an opening-up. What happens with singing, at this deep level, takes place in a way that is every bit as real—sometimes more real because of the absence of text and the diminution of purely cerebral activity— when it comes to instrumental music.

INSTRUMENTALISTS

The Catholic Church's official documents on sacred music have said a lot in recent times about instruments,[3] but very little about instrumentalists. The documents have concentrated on which instruments were suitable for the liturgy and have stated that the others were not suitable. We have had to wait a long time for any mention of the human attitude which is the principal determining factor in the use, for better or worse, of what are quite correctly known as "the instruments."

When musicians play in a small group, in a band or in an orchestra, they do not act in quite the same way as they do when they are playing by themselves, for themselves, or at home. The kind of cohesion presupposed by chamber music, for example, requires of each partner a more subtle commitment, a readiness to discern what the others are feeling and expressing in order to join with them in a rather intimate way. This union presupposes a perfect technique, but above all a communion of spirit that is indispensable for unity in interpretation. This rule, valid for all music where more than one player is involved, is of primary importance in a liturgical action because everything that happens in such an action is by its very nature communal.

So it is that instrumentalists who come to make music in the course of a celebration have a good chance of improving their role

---

3. Constitution on the Sacred Liturgy, no. 121. The Instruction on Music in the Sacred Liturgy devotes five sections to instruments (nos. 62-66) before dealing with instrumentalists in no. 67.

if they feel themselves to be genuine members of the celebrating community and if they make an effort to integrate themselves into the assembly. In this way they can live out their contributions as elements within a vast action, not limited simply to musical products.

All this is equally true of composers. Generally they succeed best when writing for an assembly that they know: not just an assembly whose musical aptitudes they are familiar with but an assembly of which they are members, an assembly from within which they live out the relationships, the depths, and the boundaries and whose limitations and barriers they have also plumbed. They compose much better when they themselves have already taken part in the meditation, the petitioning, the praise of this assembly, for they can feel in what way their brothers and sisters in the faith can best translate these basic attitudes of prayer.[4]

This does not mean that we want to exclude absolutely the collaboration of musicians who are strangers to the community, or even unbelievers, if they accept "the rules of the game"—if they are capable, in particular, of understanding or rather of feeling from within, with sympathy and respect, the deep expectations of the believers gathered together. If in practice this remains superficial and formal, it will not last. But if, on the other hand, it is lived out deeply enough to be authentic, then it has a good chance of leading those involved to a real communion of spirit.

NEW PATHWAYS

Many musicians, especially organists, are afraid that today's liturgy will take their role away from them.

Certainly the liturgical reform has now transferred into the realm of the unthinkable those Masses which until recently served as a pretext for free organ recitals.[5] But this justifiable suppression

---

4. In the United States composers have gathered with liturgists every two or three years since 1982 for extensive discussion about the direction of liturgical composition in the United States. A report on these gatherings has been published: *The Milwaukee Symposia for Church Composers: A Ten-Year Report* (Washington, DC: The Pastoral Press, 1992; Chicago: Liturgy Training Publications, 1992). Compositions have developed for parochial and cathedral settings, regional and national use. The issue of universality and unity expressed through music is consistently reexamined.

of an abuse—which only benefitted a small number of musicians and music-lovers—has been largely compensated for in the new openings that have been offered to the musician-believer: access to the richest repertoire, both ancient and modern, but also being called to improvisation, creation, to the facility of being able to adapt to the moment and to the time-span. No musician endowed with imagination can fail to rejoice at these new musical needs, these new demands, for in them will be found precisely the type of fertile constraints which favor a true freedom in creativity.

In England, the Composers' Group of the Society of St. Gregory (formerly of the Church Music Association) has met three or four times a year since November 1970 for discussion, substantial input, and most importantly evaluation of each other's work. The perceivable improvement in participants' compositional standards over the years has been very marked.

Since the mid-1970s, a number of countries—including England, France and the United States, have benefited from the work of national groupings of monastic composers and musicians.

5. This is especially true of the French tradition of organ-playing at Mass, where improvised music "covered" much of the action and players were noted for their skill in this regard. The music was at its best when based on Gregorian chant (e.g., much of the music of Tournemire, which is nothing so much as written-down improvisations). More recently, Olivier Messaien sprang from this tradition (and continued it in his church—La Trinité—in Paris) but without using Gregorian chant as a basis. In the hands of a lesser exponent, this practice could sometimes take on the dimensions cited by a contributor to *The Musical Times* in the early 1960s who complained that his ears were assaulted by "bleeding hunks of Liszt" throughout Mass at Notre Dame in Paris.

7

Ritual Functions

The presence of music in every culture—or, indeed, in the arts as a whole—suffices to prove the importance of music for humankind. Music appears as a normal manifestation of living persons. The song of a shepherd out on the mountainside is a rendition of that kind of inebriation with freedom that solitude in the midst of nature tends to produce. When a child is happy, he or she makes up a little song and starts to dance. When a group of friends gathers together for festivities or for the joy of simply being together, they often naturally express their unity by means of a song.

In very different forms, this need for sung expression is to be found in every civilization and in every age. In fact it appears as a constant, even if music *praxis* (as we will see) is not limited solely to the *raison d'être* that we have just described.

What varies from one civilization or age to another is the meaning and the place given to music; for "pure music," music launched freely into space or a void without any effect, does not exist (GL 41, p. 151). Whether we are singing or playing an instrumental piece, something is always happening. Whether you play music for your own pleasure or make use of it to create states of mind, to transmit a message, or facilitate its memorization, to allow a group to draw closer together in the pursuit of its own expression, to create ambience or to make people dance, the act of music-making always strives for some effect or other, whether we are conscious of it or not. We have even been able to analyze the effects of music on human beings, animals, and plants, and to research into its therapeutic uses.

GOING BEYOND LABELS

The relationship between music in worship and music outside worship differs considerably from one region to another. Even at the very bosom of Christianity, this relationship has greatly evolved throughout the the centuries (see GL 46 and 5, pp. 159 and 118).

Much has been said and written about the boundary separating sacred music from profane music. We have done rather less work on what it is that constitutes the *raison d'être* of music used in Christian liturgy and its mode of functioning. In this chapter we have reached the heart of the problem, for the overall thrust of the *Universa Laus* document tries to answer the fundamental question: "Why and how should one make music in the liturgy?" Defining the "ritual function" of music is exactly the same thing as answering this question.

In liturgy, as in other areas of life, music is used for widely differing purposes. Using terms strongly influenced by a tradition that arose in the last century, but whose meaning is nevertheless easily understood, the Constitution on the Liturgy defines the triple function of liturgical music as follows:

"Adding delight to prayer, fostering oneness of spirit, investing the rites with greater solemnity." This well corresponds to the three principal functions that we discover in liturgical musical practice (GL 17, p. 127):

1) Expressing what we live, in other words the faith contained in the texts and the sentiments that they evoke (GL 48, p. 163).

2) Reinforcing the sense of cohesion of the group gathered together, a function sought after since the very birth of Christianity, the unison of voices being a sign of unanimity of hearts (GL 52, p. 166).

3) Being a sign of festivity, by means of sung or instrumental pieces that correspond to the atmosphere of the liturgical season or the liturgical moment, and which reveal the freely-given nature characterizing all liturgy because it constitutes an essential element of festivity (GL 13, p. 124).

As well as these general functions, musical *praxis* can fulfil more specialized functions, as already indicated: give a certain stamp to processional movement, create a recollective atmosphere conducive to meditation, facilitate the memorization of certain texts.

A clear understanding of the ends and the means allows the composer to adopt an adequate form and an appropriate style; such an understanding facilitates the choices to be made by those drawing up orders of service; it helps those responsible for implementing orders of service to find the most propitious pace, tessitura, and interpretation.

A Dual Functionality

All these problems, however, do not resolve themselves as easily as the above statements would lead one to believe since, with art, we are always faced with multiple imponderables.

In fact we can distinguish two orders of functionality. First, we must clearly define what we are aiming at by the use of a particular musical element, and we must try to ascertain if the achieved result corresponds to what was intended. But this search for a precise goal leaves the door open for a second category of effects, greatly varied in their nature and very often difficult to perceive and to measure. This symbolical function of music, as we will see below, constitutes one of music's most important roles.

What Can be Foreseen and Is Measurable "Post Factum"

Staging a theatrical work presupposes the involvement of several people: an author, a stage manager and a producer, some actors, the house manager, a publicity manager, someone in charge of painting and creating stage sets, wardrobe manager, etc. Each person fulfills a determinable function, distinct from that of the others, but all of them have the realization of the same work as their aim. Each one, within the specific area of his or her contribution, is aiming at a precise goal and awaits the realization of that goal.

The same is true for celebration. Among those responsible for the liturgy, the musicians play a determinable role, taking into account the totality of the liturgical action, in respect of which they "orientate" all their contributions. In order to carry out their task correctly, they are not content merely to look after the music that they are creating, that they have chosen, or that they are performing: they know that this music will not attain its true fullness unless it can be organically integrated into the celebration considered as a whole, and they know that this music must be linked to the celebration with multiple bonds of all kinds. The function of each musical element determines its form and its execution.

For this to happen, musicians must have knowledge of the whole gamut of vocal acts and liturgical rites. Each liturgical act that makes use of music requires a particular form of music which is appropriate to that act, and this at a number of different levels:

1) Through the form being best suited to the rite that it is serving:

The word "litany" represents a very precise kind of form, invocation and refrain; a processional calls for a regular rhythm and extends over a certain period of time; the refrain of a penitential rite must be able to integrate itself with that rite, and the refrain of the general intercessions should be composed and selected with regard to the intentions that precede it; an organist does not thoughtlessly play the same piece for a time of meditation as for a recessional (GL 45, p. 158).

2) Through the genre and style allowing what is envisaged actually to come to life:

An acclamation needs a form that has a certain vigor about it; a prayer such as the Our Father, on the other hand, needs a musical sobriety that will allow interiorization to happen; expressing praise calls for a melody imbued with lyricism; psalm-singing makes use of various forms depending on the character of the text; the simple dialogue between presider and assembly requires formulas that are organically linked to each other. In each case, the character of the music must be adapted to the atmosphere of the text and the atmosphere of the rite, without which this music cannot be validly integrated into the liturgy.

3) Through the performers and their performance:

A celebrant, a psalmist, a choir, an assembly cannot perform different kinds of music with indifference as if these types of music were all exactly the same. They have to take into account the proper role of whatever kind of music it is. There is also the whole question of physical posture—standing, sitting, walking—which can greatly affect the way in which a particular piece functions.

Because we have not always hitherto been sufficiently sensitive to this type of demand, the result has been a gradual gulf between

music and liturgy, music often appearing as a decorative acces-
sory and independent of the rite.

The rediscovery of the link with the liturgy is an exceptional
opportunity for thinking musicians. It allows them to envisage a
kind of music that is appropriate for the rite, and offers them a
certain number of criteria for analyzing and evaluating *post factum*
the way in which the music "functioned."

GOING BEYOND ANALYSIS

Our academic knowledge—especially about the fundamental
laws of the functioning of music in a given cultural milieu—can
explain certain phenomena and allow us to plan ahead; but this
knowledge also always leaves the door open to the unforeseeable
and the imponderable. All church musicians therefore need to
have, alongside their knowledge, a sensitivity that has been finely-
honed in the school of experience.

Through sensitivity they come to discern what people like to
sing, what creates an atmosphere of festive joy, or recollection, or
quietening down—all of which can create unity within a rite or
within an overall celebration. They see born in themselves, little by
little, a certain flair which allows them to gauge skilfully how to
renew the repertoire in use by avoiding staleness as well as
insecurity. In this order of things, a sensitivity that is attentive,
guided, and sustained by intelligent analysis, can allow us to press
further ahead and to go beyond the banal application of rubrics
and recipes.

But even when we have reached this stage, surprises and
question-marks continually arise. Some of us lose our courage and
our desire to move forward, whereas others are able to realize that
this can simply be a sign that we have gone too far too fast rather
than a signal to stop.

In fact, when precisely-formulated rules and regulations have
provided the service that we can expect of them, when sensitivity
has allowed us to live things out in their deepest essence, there still
remains a whole mysterious and uncontrollable domain which is
nevertheless real. We discover this when a completely different
atmosphere from the one we had in mind is created, or when
people reject what we like or are enthusiastic about what we do not
like, or when there is a feeling of oneness, or communion, or

something else altogether which we had not foreseen (GL 57, p. 169).

Saying this should not bring us up short, as if against a wall, but on the contrary should be for us a sign of opening-up, as if it were a sign that the liturgical act is not closed in on itself but, rather, ceaselessly calls us to a going beyond ourselves which will give it its own meaning and value.

This is a real liturgical opportunity: through such a "mysterious" experience, unsuspected horizons can be opened up. At this point music plays an irreplaceable role since it is precisely here where words and explanations flounder and reach their limits that new terrains can be seen leading on to the unknown. From this point on, it is not possible to measure or control what is happening, and there will be as many different reactions as there are people involved in living out the experience. Nevertheless, something is happening which the rite cannot and must not try to enclose between retaining walls, but instead must leave the field open to personal choice and the action of the Spirit.

This mysterious reality demands much discretion and humility from musicians. Sensing the effect that might be obtainable at this point, a young composer recently renounced certain musical procedures precisely out of a fear of manipulating people's sensibilities with the power of his music.

Even here, music must retain its role, even though its risks and limitations are understood. A liturgical text already, by itself, generates an infinity of images and meanings. Music goes even further and thus becomes, whether or not a text is present, a sign of invisible and untranslatable realities—the very realities the believer is celebrating. Music carries us beyond words, and this is why vocalises, instrumental pieces, the subtlest nuances, and the strangest timbres can find their place in the liturgy, since they create that space which opens us up to silence.

With such a rich field of possibilities for action before them, musicians have two pathways to follow.

They can either move in the direction of the determinate, of "closedness," orientating choices and limiting possible meanings. For example, a very expressive psalm-melody forces the performer and the listeners to grasp first and foremost the meaning that the composer decided to express. A triumphant *Sanctus* with trumpets and a measured rhythmical tread makes us feel that this piece is an acclamation, almost a confession of faith.

But composers can also opt for the indeterminate, for openness, for a plurality of meanings, for freedom of choice left to performers and listeners from among many possible directions. A melodic formula with very discreet inflection leaves open the possibility that the text may be absorbed in different ways. Similarly, a meditative and "adorational" *Sanctus* can, by the very fact of introducing something rather different from what we are used to, invite us to live out the same text in a way that is quite new.

In opting for this second direction, musicians are promoting the order of the symbolic. We can glimpse what new dimensions the "liturgical functionality" of a musical piece might take on . . .

MUSIC OF THE WHOLE PERSON

These two orders of functionality coexist in liturgy: there is always something verifiable which allows us to reflect, to ask questions and provide answers; and there is always something which remains indecisive, even mysterious.

Furthermore, the two areas interpenetrate each other and have a reciprocal influence on each other. It is not possible to have ritual music without functionality. Art for art's sake has no place in liturgy. The other side of the coin is that all ritual music, however "functional" it may be, always wriggles out of being totally determinable. It is one of the special "places" where the perpetual newness of the mystery celebrated is created and manifested.

So we have had a glimpse of the astonishing complexity of musical phenomena. This is a difficult exercise, but it is a great opportunity for the musicians, for here they will find an immense field of freedom freely given. In this way their music will be able to signify the gift given by humankind, and the way we freely and without reservation hold on to God's invitation, in the fraternal communion of the church in openness to the world.

We can analyze any kind of music and tease out its rhythms and its tonalities: and yet it will still carry us beyond itself, leading us through the interplay of symbols until we are not only carried beyond the music but beyond our very selves. In its complexity, music accompanies humankind on its journey, in its actions, in its listening to the word, and in its response, its effort to open itself up to the Lord: humankind complete—body, heart and spirit (GL 16, p. 126).

8

Repertoires and Models

When church musicians speak about their art, they are often thinking about repertoire, about their collections of hymnals, octavos, and songbooks. Nevertheless, they are well aware that all this paper only exists in relation to its performance. A musical work, whatever it may be, only becomes a reality in the act which, time after time, re-creates it. The music may certainly resound in the creative imagination of its composer, but it only reaches its true state on the day that one or several performers create it and hear it. Transcribed onto paper, it can be multiplied thousands of times over, but it only becomes music by means of the "sonic act" that gives it life.

This is true for all music, but for ritual music it is an even more demanding precondition because simply producing the sounds of the music is not sufficient to make a musical work into a liturgical piece. The work needs to enter into the totality of an action, and it is as a musical "gesture," as an act and as part of the liturgical act that it finds its true meaning. Indeed, in the liturgy music is not an additional décor, a sort of theater music that inserts interludes between the different phases of the celebration. Singing and music are integrated into the liturgy itself, liturgy which is "act." Therefore it is first and foremost in the realm of action that music finds its place among the elements in a celebration (GL 25, p. 133).

It is possible to conceive of other extra-liturgical attitudes to this kind of music which might be encountered, but these other ways of using it remain secondary with respect to the primary act. For example, it is possible to listen to a recording of liturgical music just like any other recording, but this music only acquires its total meaning within the ritual action for which it is designed. Recordings and sheet music allow other communities to have knowledge of what a composer and a community have created on an initial occasion, and so they are very useful for transmitting repertoire to others; but the whole purpose is that other assemblies may in turn be able to draw out of them a new musical act for their own celebrations.

CREATION AND MEMORY

If the realm of action is primary in liturgy, every musical performance must be lived out as a creation or a re-creation. However, it would be unthinkable to want every piece at every liturgy to spring spontaneously from the fertile imagination of a composer present in the assembly. The creative musical act is only possible in a historical context and in a cultural context. It demands a long gestation period and this charism presupposes a relatively rare manifestation of itself in practice.

It would not only be unthinkable but also incomplete. By the very nature of the rite, the participants must be able to be part of the rite by finding themselves in a familiar context. To do this, they need to use, several times over, gestures and words and well-known songs which, through slow assimilation, can become their own prayer. In order to be able to recognize the particular atmosphere of a feast or a liturgical season, they also need to re-use and re-hear certain pieces that are characteristic of these occasions and are reserved for such occasions like precious jewels from one year to the next.

This is the way in which, at different times in the history of the church and in different cultures, ritual music repertoires were built up, signs both of the fertility of their source and the diversity of their impact on the cultures in which they were born.

Moreover, calling on memory and repetition corresponds to a fundamental characteristic of liturgy, which is in essence the memorial of Christ's sacrifice, renewed and re-actualized in every celebration. This "re" prefix of itself evokes the need for continually taking many different well-known and familiar elements in order to create the live wire which links all these celebrations together. Thus repetition becomes a sign of this memorial, becomes a symbolic proclamation of that mysterious reality, ever-new and always to come, which is God's life for the family of believers.

USING EXISTING REPERTOIRES

From another point of view, the need to call on existing repertoires derives from a number of very concrete reasons.

In order for an assembly really to take part in the singing, in order for it to be able to respond to a soloist in a sung or spoken dialogue, it is necessary for the formulas to be known by everyone. Only brief reprises (GL 44, p. 158) integrated into a psalm or a litany can offer the means for immediate participation that needs no preparation. Beyond this, the words and the melody carrying them must form part of a repertoire that is not only known but also absorbed into one's being. Singing the *Sanctus*—so important in the unfolding of the great eucharistic prayer—is a good illustration of this requirement: its relatively long text does not allow a parish-type community to change the melody too often; and the very atmosphere within which it should be sung, following the presider's invitation, demands that it be possible to take part in it fully, joyously, and immediately.

This necessity for calling on well-known formulae even goes further than repertoire; it is concretized in the way in which the repertoire is actually used. If we want the assembly to respond to the invitation in a dialogue, or to take up an antiphon sung by a soloist or a choir, the way in which the elements are linked must always be exactly identical so that the "habit" of responding is not troubled by any kind of hesitation. In a situation where several different cantors take it in turn to lead the assembly Sunday after Sunday, it is important that their way of eliciting a response from the assembly be essentially the same, for the smallest difference can give rise to unsureness and hesitation. In other words, we are looking for a certain stability in repertoire and in the way the repertoire is used.

The use of existing repertoires is also demanded by other considerations. Certain masterworks, according to the judgment of our experience, carry with them a unique atmosphere simply by reason of their intrinsic value. Their form is acknowledged to be very close to perfection. Consequently, they can be integrated at certain points in a celebration, and bring to that celebration a substance that other less perfect pieces could not.

There also exist works permeated with connotations, difficult to analyze, but closely linked to widely-shared affective or spiritual experiences; and this enables them to be part of a particular repertoire because of that mysterious power that they possess which acts on our sensibilities. The history of liturgy includes cases—like the responsory *Media Vita* (GL 28, p. 137)—where the impact of the piece was so strong that eventually people ascribed almost magical powers to it. In certain churches, it has been found that a motet like Vittoria's *O Vos Omnes* produces a particular kind of atmosphere, and so its use is reserved for particular circumstances when this kind of atmosphere is required. In other situations, the Midnight Mass "theme music" has turned out to be a rather sentimental Christmas carol, however ghastly we may think its text and music to be. When the triple Alleluia resounds through the paschal night, it is actually in itself announcing the Resurrection, even if its text—the single word Alleluia—is used throughout most of the rest of the year. Our assemblies await these musical signals, and those responsible for drawing up musical programs must be careful to preserve them from being devalued by only using them at moments where they can fully carry out their role.

REPETITION AND NEWNESS THROUGH USING THE OPERATIVE MODEL

Liturgy therefore needs new elements at the same time as it needs familiar ones. The rite as it is lived is both stability and newness, tradition and creation. Theoretically, we could respond to this double demand by alternately using well-known works and newly-created ones.

But the liturgy integrates this dual requirement in a single reality, through the use of the "operative musical model." (GL 33, p. 142)

Here we are talking about a simple basic formula, easily recognizable and memorizable, with a structure that is flexible enough to allow multiple adaptations to new texts, but which also leaves a relatively large amount of freedom to the performer, especially if the performer is a soloist.

Without being a highly qualified musician, a presider with normal gifts can improvise the cantillation (see GL 7, p. 120) of a preface when given a preface tone as a model. Beginner psalmists need to write down the basic formula on which to perform the verses, but they quickly become capable of constructing psalmody by themselves if they know the structure of the text and the rules for a good melodic link back to the response. The use of Byzantine-Slavic-type models allows an entire group to improvise simple polyphony by starting from linking together a few well-known chords.

Such practices are very valuable for the liturgy. Solo singers should at least be trained to use several different models of the recitative type since this allows them to bring to the celebration precisely that element of newness needed by the celebration, without having to go to the trouble of writing out some elaborate creation or other.

Perhaps this is the point at which to draw attention to a danger to be avoided: the temptation to move away from the model in order to produce something original. The development of the gradual psalm in late Gregorian chant is a good example of what can happen when basic psalmody is left to a soloist. In the beginning, this kind of psalmody simply used the model: the basic formula was certainly easily grasped, and its development integrated a certain number of centonized (GL 8, p. 120) melodic cells. The soloist brought all these elements together so as to produce a melody that was both recognizable and always new. But little by little the skill of psalmists carried them further and further away from a concern for the text. The result was the development of extremely ornate pieces where the soloist showed off his virtuosity, rather similar to the way in which a later generation of instrumental soloists would show off in concerto cadenzas. In analyzing plainchant graduals it is often quite difficult to discover the original tone that carried the psalmody and that served as a model for this generous flowering of notes. At the same time, it is also rather difficult to follow the text.

Today, if we invite soloists to exercise more freedom by the use of operative models, it is important that they also know how to keep this form of singing within bounds without which the singing loses its rationale. But we can easily imagine the many advantages of a correct use of operative models.

We have looked at three cases where soloists or groups could without difficulty bring a certain newness to celebration in this way. The psalmody of the office, as well as certain short responsories, are used in religious communities in a similar way. They help us to measure the great flexibility and at the same time the relative ease of use of this type of formula—familiar, quickly grasped, not distracting by difficulty nor by over-expressiveness.

At the same time, a model that is used well brings a constant newness with it, because of the adaptation which is inherent in it. In particular, it gives the soloist an easy way of proclaiming a text while allowing that soloist all the freedom necessary for correct expression and a proper production of the accentuation and structure of each phrase. However, the formula wisely puts a limit on the dangers of running into personal expression that is too theatricalized.

By using the operative model, the text that is proclaimed or meditated upon takes on a form sufficiently familiar not to distract by its originality, and at the same time the text is adorned each time with enough newness to avoid routine. By this very fact, the text can signify that the liturgical act of which it forms part is a unique moment rather than the mere replaying of a rite that is fixed for ever.

Toward Harmonious Balance

In liturgical music, as in many other fields, it is the exclusive searching for a recognized and appreciated value which provokes tensions and misunderstandings. When it is possible to take in the totality of the values involved, it is easier to achieve the right mixture, avoiding both absolutes and exclusivities.

However, there certainly exists a very convenient solution which was often adopted in the course of history and which eliminates numerous problems: this solution is the imposition of an unchangeable ritual repertoire. But this solution has become almost unthinkable in today's actual context. Now, the situation itself imposes choices on us.

If we are only concerned with promoting easy participation in liturgical singing, we run the risk of limiting ourselves to a few well-known refrain formulas or short acclamations. If we are only concerned with aesthetic value, we are tempted to entrust all the musical elements to trained soloists, to a competent choir, to first-class instrumentalists; and we are tempted to construct programs by delving exclusively into the most classical of repertoires. If we are only concerned with creativity, we open ourselves up to the danger of rapid exhaustion since no community can very long endure a continual flood of new pieces.

It is in a correct balance, adapted to the actual resources available (a composer, a soloist capable of singing free psalmody, a choir trained in the performance of one kind of repertoire or another, a skilled animator for educating and leading the assembly), that the liturgy team will find a concrete solution for each situation, taking into account the reactions (both previous and foreseeable) of the faithful.

The criteria brought into play need to be broad enough to respond as well as possible to the diverse expectations of the assembly, whether these expectations are conscious or unconscious, articulated or simply conjectured. As we will see shortly, it is not a case of following the latest fashion or of trivializing the music but of finding within the rich diversity of possible forms a balance broad enough to respond to the diversity of needs. And this is something that only an educated, open, and attentive liturgy team can provide.

9

Quality and Value of Forms

CONCERN FOR QUALITY

We tend to reproach some of those responsible for drawing up programs of liturgical music with "putting on anything, no matter what." This criticism springs from a demand for quality, linked to a particular idea of what we should be doing with liturgy.

Moreover, this is not a new concern. We find it frequently expressed throughout the history of liturgy. If it occurs more frequently today than thirty years ago, this is quite simply because of the changes that have taken place since the council. When the basic repertoire was fixed and untouchable, the problem was limited to a few choices in the field of polyphonic repertoires and, outside the eucharist, in the area of hymns of greater or lesser popularity. However, the principle of certain demands in the choice of works and their interpretation was real and universal.

Opinions as to quality are always diverse, always relative. Essentially they depend on cultural habits, in particular on the musical repertoires used in the geographical area in question, on the formation provided in schools, on the musical *praxis* of groups of amateurs and professionals, and (even more today) on the fashions imposed by the media.

The demands that are formulated for ritual music can be reduced to two[1] basic categories:

---

1. In the United States the Bishops' Committee on the Liturgy's document Music in Catholic Worship, published in 1972, has served to

(a) The first group of criteria relate to aesthetic value: Is the music "beautiful" in itself? Does it bring to the performers themselves as well as to the listeners that "interior uplifting," that aesthetic joy expected from an authentic work of art? Is it well performed? In all these questions, the focus is on the value of the musical elements.

(b) The second group of criteria is more directly connected with the relationship of these elements to the liturgy: Are they appropriate for "helping people to pray" according to the different traditional modes of Christian prayer? Do they create an atmosphere favorable to the full accomplishment of the liturgical action, both overall and at any particular moment? Are they "worthy" of the celebration?

This dual set of demands is expressed just as much in the official documents of the church (GL 9, p. 121) as in the reflections of the faithful. As for musicians, they mostly insist on the first aspect. Especially during the last few years the positions musicians espouse are based on a desire to see an end to the proliferation of types of music which they judge to be mediocre and therefore unworthy of the liturgy—and of their art.

DIFFICULTIES INHERENT IN A SCALE OF VALUES

"Beauty," "piety," and "dignity" are positive criteria. But when we come to grips with the concrete application of these principles we find criticisms formulated in a negative way in the vast majority of cases: it is the absence or insufficiency of the above-mentioned qualities which is most often the object of the criticism.

The performance of "anything, no matter what" in the course of liturgy cannot be permitted, and this is also aimed as much at the absence of any aesthetic value—a notion that is often extremely vague, and related to the (very variable) musical culture of the persons doing the talking—as at the absence of conformity to a certain way of celebrating. In fact these two demands are normally linked together in the following thought-process: any kind of

---

guide pastoral musicians in the direction of a threefold judgment: a musical, a liturgical, and a pastoral judgment. The material presented by *Universa Laus* combines the liturgical and pastoral judgment into one: "are they appropriate for 'helping people to pray'?"

music judged to be "not beautiful" is therefore incapable of "promoting the conditions for prayer."

It is difficult to do precise research in areas where so many factors, known or unsuspected, come into play at one time, and where the kind of vocabulary used by the different speakers already suffers from a terrible lack of precision. In particular, the term "sacred music," as we have already seen, is an extremely ambiguous one (see GL 46, p. 159).

According to their level of faith and their particular way of praying, all individuals have a particular concept of the liturgical action, and thus of the types of music that can be integrated into it. It is also true that there are areas of the world where music traditionally holds a higher place than elsewhere, where people are more willing to sing than elsewhere, where spontaneously bursting into song is more common than elsewhere, where festivity is expressed more commonly by dancing, shouting for joy, and the use of instruments than elsewhere.

It is simply not possible to translate into terms of a few all-purpose formulas all the expectations and the criticisms of believers throughout the world, even if it is clear that there is a large measure of agreement on the need for quality.

LISTENING TO NON-SPECIALISTS

If it is sometimes difficult to discern with exactitude the demands made by musicians and liturgists, it is even more difficult to gain a realization of the judgments of the faithful. Nevertheless, comparatively few of the faithful are insensitive to music or indifferent to the musical menu served up for them in their churches. Praise and complaint are often heard, but these judgments are only rarely formulated in a way that is both precise and susceptible of analysis. Normally, rather vague expressions are used: "It was beautiful!" or "It was awful!"—without any indication being given as to why this opinion is held. Is it the work itself? Or its melody? Or its text? Its accompaniment? Was it the performance? Or the quality of the voices or instruments? Was it because of the sound system? Or the general atmosphere created by the music?

Those responsible for celebrations may be tempted to set aside such imprecisely formulated reflections on the part of nonexperts. Nevertheless, if those responsible want to be of real service to the community they must force themselves, patiently and persistently, to understand what the members of the assembly are trying to say. They must try to perceive, through the dark glass of vague and stereotyped expressions, the real point which helped or hindered the prayer of those who are speaking.

Very often they will get very different reactions to the same piece in the same celebration. This obviously comes from the diversity of people, from their concentration on one particular element or another, from the overall context which helped or annihilated the use of a musical element at a particular point. It is therefore impossible to arrive at one clear and simple idea representing the reactions of the assembly; but it is in a very humble way, using intuition rather than rigorous deduction, that they will come to sense what the members of an assembly are comfortable with.

A Mean Average or a Space Filled with Potential?

Looking at this from another angle, a mean average is never a sufficient and definite criterion for judgment, since it always levels out the differences, excluding by definition the most precise and the most trenchant opinions. If a concern for obtaining an "honest average" is legitimate in itself, there is always the risk of coloration by passing fashions, or the risk of insipid or lifeless routine. And if ritual music must accompany and serve an action that involves the participants in a quite different way from a comforting lullaby, then the music often benefits by bringing a sense of contrast, even the effect of surprise, and thus of the "new song" desired by the psalmist, in order to signify the "new person" put forward by the Gospel.

It is difficult to find the right balance between, on the one hand, this desire for a kind of music that is capable of drawing forth or supporting the radical conversion demanded of every believer and, on the other hand, the necessity of limiting signs of renewal by regulating them according to the degree of receptivity of the believers gathered together. Being able to recognize a "working space" that is appropriate for the whole enterprise, or being able to discern the frontiers beyond which we risk meeting rejection or alienation—all this is part of a certain wisdom which is a form of charity.

This is an extended effort which we should not be undertaking on our own but which presupposes a contribution based on different kinds of sensitivities—sensitivities which will be attentive to the most tenuous reactions, to silences, to certain hesitations on the part of the assembly, in order to serve that assembly better by offering the assembly forms of expression that it can assimilate and which at the same time ceaselessly call it to go beyond itself.

Study days and magazine articles cannot resolve this concrete problem, and our most scientific analyses begin by making us prudent in our judgments and in our evaluation of the judgments of others. They show us that nothing can be settled by theories and that it is in the concrete actuality of celebration that true discernment takes place.

ART AND ITS CONTEXT: A DUAL REQUIREMENT

At this level no principle for evaluation, no criterion can be applied by itself, for everything that is perceived is linked to the multiple circumstances of time and place, atmosphere and cultural habits within which the celebration occurs: large church/small church/open air; morning liturgy/evening celebration; large diverse assembly/small homogeneous group; festive/routine/boring atmosphere; organic placement of musical elements in the overall ritual context/accidental contribution of background music; timbres in conformity with the demands of the listeners/timbres that shock their ears; performance suitable/not suitable to the degree of interiorization/festiveness of the whole.

Multiple variables contribute to each celebration. We need to learn little by little how to discern them so that we can have a greater knowledge of them and tease out the elements that it is possible to improve upon.

Patience, attentiveness, wisdom, humility: these human qualities are all as indispensable for ritual musical practice as technical competence, artistic quality, and theoretical knowledge.

But the ones do not go without the others. Goodwill and a pastoral sense by themselves are not sufficient. Too often, the most laudable of intentions end in negative results, discouraging both musicians and the faithful who are concerned about a certain quality in liturgy. Holding art in contempt, trial and error, a do-it-yourself approach—all these inevitably compromise the anticipated result.

We need to reach the point of being able to bring into mutual agreement, mutual harmony, cross-fertilization the consciousness of the assembly and the quality of the musical forms used. Liturgy in its totality is an art. It is not by refusing the fundamental demands of art that we will bring about good celebrations but, on the contrary, by respecting these demands through a close and trusting collaboration between liturgists and musicians.

10

Signifying a New Humanity

Western society as a whole is currently in the midst of a profound cultural change, and the institutional churches are not managing to avoid it. In this context it is inevitable that numerous misunderstandings about singing and instrumental music are being raised. Most often they can be explained in the light of too limited a vision of the problems.

The majority of the tensions could be dissipated by a return to the essential, which is this: the basic thing that is being asked of ritual music is that it should respond to the actual goal of the liturgical action. Now, the liturgy is pursuing a double aim:

• to express the faith of the assembled believers, their waiting for the Kingdom of God whose realization, always present and always looked for, will only be fully accomplished (as they know) at the end of time (see GL 21, p. 129);

• to achieve each time a further step forward on the road to that birth of the new humanity towards which every Christian moves by participating in the eucharist and thus participating in the death and resurrection of Christ (GL 32, p. 141).

It is in light of this dual requirement that all liturgical music should be evaluated. We can easily see the principal difficulty: how can we speak, how can we sing something that we only live in a very imperfect way? Whether they be composers or performers, church musicians—like all other Christians—are also part of this slow march of progress. Those who are furthest along the way will still feel that the goal is very far off; others will perceive it as a very vague ideal; and others will not even have glimpsed this perspective and will thus be content with musical or liturgical criteria of a purely formal nature. Of these three groups of musicians, only the first will have any chance of grasping the problem, since their own interior growth will allow them at least to perceive the goal and the pathways of such a journey. The discovery of this dual basic requirement of all liturgy is only obtained at the price of a long period of self-discipline, which is itself inscribed in the "mutation" of a being who is transformed by a faith lived out in depth and in the truth of every moment.

Musical value, whether it be endorsed by immediate general appreciation (attribution as a "hit") or by being recognized as devoted to the secular world, constitutes an important criterion for judgment, and moreover one that is so deeply rooted in our cultural customs that it would be unthinkable simply to ignore it. Liturgical value—i.e., the suitability of a musical piece to be an organic element of the celebration—represents another criterion that is equally indispensable if we are to make a correct judgment.

But these two orders of value reach their fullness when they are placed and integrated into the overall liturgical enterprise and allow Christians gathered together to cry out in supplication to this God who gives them awareness of their limitations and a voice to make them known, to sing out their thanksgiving for the victory of the forces of life over those of death and evil (a victory achieved in Christ, the firstborn from the dead, and in that part of themselves already renewed by grace), and lastly to convey their waiting in joyful hope for the day when the Kingdom of God will be accomplished in all its fullness.

THE ONLY TRUE CRITERION

We have to understand this dimension in all its power and in all its radicalness, for it will certainly allow us to resolve all the tensions and leave behind all the opposing points of view, even those that are based on very deep and highly respectable cultural criteria.

The real criterion actually becomes the suitability of a type of music to promote in human beings this openness to what is beyond us and to what, paradoxically, gives us our true dimension as human beings. This transformation is so complete—if it were not, how could we talk about death and resurrection?—that it can work through pathways that are extremely diverse and unforeseeable, and can be translated musically in many different ways: by the stripping-down that takes place with types of music that are absolutely simple and have become signs of that poverty without which we cannot discover the richness of the Kingdom; by the bubbling-up in sound of a profusion of voices and instrumental timbres whose pluralism harmonized into unity becomes a sign of that superabundance to which all believers are invited.

In either case, and in the whole gamut of intermediate situations imaginable, music opens up human beings, it helps them transcend themselves and their development. The only type of music which by its very nature should be excluded from the liturgical action is a type of music that brings human beings back to their own diminutive stature, that folds them in on themselves instead of spreading them wide, expanding them to the dimensions of the new humanity announced by the Gospel. How can we "ex-press" ourselves, how can we give praise to and entreat Someone infinitely other, how can we participate in the life of the community—if we are turned in on our own image? This attitude is of its nature excluded from the liturgy.

Towards "Universa Laus"

Universa Laus, the name chosen by this international group, is significant. In itself it constitutes the expression of a utopia, one which consists of waiting for the day when every creature will participate in universal praise in the Kingdom that has at last been accomplished: a utopia because not a single one of us will see its realization in this life and because many generations have yet to pass before such a hope flourishes in reality.

But this utopia is at the same time the surest of hopes for the disciples of the Risen One; for the way has been open since the day when the psalmist invited humankind to sing a new song (Ps 32:3; 39:4; 95:1; 97:1; 149:1). This way was followed by the uncountable singing procession of the Elect in the Book of Revelation (21:2; 7:9-10); and twenty centuries of Christianity have accumulated thousand upon thousand of new works that have, for century after century, nourished the song of assemblies gathered in the name of Jesus Christ.

The multitude of these works, born of the creative power of musicians, offers us a wonderful image of this praise which is in a constant state of growth. Imagining an act of continual praise—whose tapestry is woven, even today, from one liturgy to another, from one religious house to another, from one continent to another, across the time zones that mark out the spinning of the globe—offers us, hour after hour, an incomparably uplifting vision.

Nevertheless, we all know how modest this praise is by comparison with the forces of self-interest and hatred which are at work in the world. If the music of the Kingdom is to burst forth, then the living force of Christian faith must act in every believer, in every community, in every church, transforming hearts and allowing them to express with ever-increasing truth that waiting for a world of justice and peace, a world of love.[1]

On the other hand, we all know that the very expression of this waiting, reinforced by the mysterious power of music acting upon all the fibers of our being, helps us to subsist on it, helps us to desire it to be more efficacious. Praise lived out in this way does not become a balm that soothes consciences, a flight from reality, but rather an inner nourishment by which every part of our being is gradually impregnated with this total praise, this *Universa Laus*.

Starting from Christian faith lived out in its fullness, at every instant of life there can be growth which is capable of progressively transforming a human environment into a region of love, creating those living cells of the Kingdom of God so often sung about and so rarely lived in reality.

In a world in the throes of transformation, in a society where interpersonal and international relations are so often marked by fear and self-interest, the gospel message must bring with it this dimension of openness and self-giving without which there can be no true relationship nor human progress. Thus from one believer to another, from one region of the world to another, little by little, can grow contacts that are more human, which will in their turn give rise to that *Universa Laus* which is our hope.

---

1. In the French original, a quotation from the song *En mémoire du Seigneur* (In Memory of the Lord) by Didier Rimaud SJ.

Part Three

Glossary

1. Active Participation (see p. 60)

No less than twelve times does the Constitution on the Sacred Liturgy of the Second Vatican Council recommend the "active" participation of the faithful in liturgical celebrations:
- in nos. 11, 14, 19, 21, 27, 30, 41, 48, 50, 79, 113, 124;
- no. 14 is the most important;
- no. 113 is devoted to singing;
- the adjective "active" is often accompanied by one of these further adjectives: "conscious," "fruitful," "full," "communal," "devotional," etc.

Such insistence is remarkable, but the demand is not new. It dates from the beginning of the century—more precisely, from Pope St. Pius X in his motu proprio *Tra le sollicitudini* of 1903.

Two erroneous interpretations often damage the full scope of this expression.

• Some believe that this means that the faithful have to do everything. This is quite untrue. In no. 28 the constitution clearly says: "In liturgical celebrations each person, minister or lay person who has an office to perform should carry out all and only those parts which pertain to his office by the nature of the rite and the liturgical norms."

• There are also those who believe that this means that the faithful must constantly be doing something exterior . . .

In reality, the "active participation" of the faithful in the liturgy means, first of all, that all the faithful—by virtue of their baptism and by virtue of the participation that this sacrament gives them in the priesthood of Christ—are active members of the celebration, and not spectators or bystanders. It is in this sense, for example, that the priest-celebrant always speaks in the first person plural, even if he is the only one speaking: "Let us pray"—"Let us give thanks"—"We have these gifts to offer"—"We offer you." At Mass, everyone celebrates.

Next, we need to be clear that this "activity" of the faithful, if it is continual during the celebration, is not constantly an exterior activity. It may well be exterior in a chant, or a common prayer (the "I confess," for example), or a procession; but it is not exterior when listening to a reading, or when uniting oneself silently to the prayer that the priest-celebrant makes in the name of the whole assembly, or when meditating with the aid of a chant sung by the choir or a piece played by the organist. It is even less exterior when everyone is silent before a prayer or after communion.

Thus the believer is called to be always active (praying, singing, listening, offering . . .) but according to modes of participation which vary according to the nature of the act.

Finally, we should say that if active participation is not ceaselessly exterior (we don't sing or move all the time), the other side of the coin is that it must be always interior. Even if there is total silence, there is never a single moment at Mass when the believer has nothing to do.

2. Anthropology (see p. 34)

(a) *A more biblical anthropology*

Breaking away from the body-soul dualism which only promotes the salvation of the latter in order to subdue the passions of the former, the *Universa Laus* document recovers the biblical concept of the unity of the entire human being who lives in a body created by God and who is animated by the breath of a spirit that comes from God.

This way of seeing and feeling harks back especially to the Book of the Psalms, so central to Christian liturgy: human beings know that their bodies are the *locus* wherein they relate to themselves, to others, and to God, and they know that their bodies are the basic instrument allowing them to sing and to make music.

(b) *A more modern anthropology*

• which is founded on the research and conclusions of the human sciences: psychoanalysis, social psychology, sociology, semiology, etc.;

• which gets away from Euro-centrism, puts the west into perspective, and takes account of the diversity of the cultures, customs, and thus of the types of music which make up each people;

• which knows that culture is the total determining factor in an individual, to the point where the individual can only think, speak, sing, make music, and be truly free in the context of that culture;

• which conceives of the unity of humanity not in a mode of uniformity (the same Gregorian chant for all Catholics and all countries!) but like a kind of polyphony, a treasure-trove of wealth, an acknowledgement of the gifts of God, and thus an acceptance of the differences and the will which those differences express, especially through instrumental music and singing.

(c) *A more biblical theology*

• which escapes from an obsession with the Fall and with sin in order to welcome God's wonderful plan in the creation which God made so that people might sing the divine glory; the plan that the Father pursues in the work of his Son Jesus Christ who came to show the way, through his death and resurrection, for humanity to attain the glory of the Father; the plan that God's church accomplishes now and until the Son's return.

(d) *A more modern theology*

• which, after Vatican II, sees in the church the sign and the sacrament of salvation for the human race, the People of God gathered to live out and proclaim to the world the liberation won by Christ, and no longer a mere grouping-together of those who by their faith will escape divine punishment;
• which does not take unto itself everything that normally comes under the heading of religion or the sacred, but which desires to convert and purify all "natural" religious initiatives in the light of faith in Jesus Christ (and it is particularly in this sense that the document prefers to speak of ritual music rather than sacred music).

3. Assembly, The (see p. 50)

The rediscovery of the meaning of the assembly is one of the most important benefits of the Second Vatican Council.

Even the best things can be eroded in the course of time, and long duration can weaken their effect or even send them off in the wrong direction altogether. So it was possible in the 1950s, when referring to "church," actually to be thinking about "pope"; and, in another area, we spoke about "assisting" at Mass. This did not prevent Christians of this era from being good members of the faithful, but it did need a serious "readjustment" or *aggiornamento* as John XXIII put it.

In fact in the New Testament and for the Fathers of the church (the great theologians of the early centuries) the church was none other than the assembly, since it was the Greek word *ekklesia* that they chose to signify the liturgical gathering of Christians (see 1 Cor 11:18). In a Greek city, the *ekklesia* was the gathering of free citizens, called together to deal with public matters.

Thus we can say that there is no church without assembly. This can be verified at the universal level—the church is the gathering of all the assemblies of the world (and the council showed that only too well)—but also at the local level. In a particular town, in a particular district, in a particular borough there is church because there are Christians who gather together.

Christians do not live constantly in assembly: they have their family life, their work, their leisure activities. But it is the assembly—and above all the Sunday assembly—which constitutes the nub of their Christian existence and which renders visible the fact that the church is alive.

If this is so, it is easy to understand why the assembly is the "primary subject" of the liturgy, which is to say that the liturgy rests in the assembly. It is so true that the assembly—from the simple fact that it exists—is a locus which actualizes the Lord's very presence. The council said this in no. 7 of the Constitution on the Sacred Liturgy, recalling the words of Jesus: "Where two or three are gathered in my name, I am there in the midst of them" (Mt 18:20); and Pope Paul VI commented on this in his Instruction on the Eucharistic Mystery (*Eucharisticum Mysterium*) of 13 April 1967:

> To enable the faithful to understand the eucharistic mystery more deeply, they should be taught the principle ways in which the Lord himself is present in the liturgical celebrations of the church.
>
> He is always present in the assembly of the faithful gathered in his name (see Mt 18:20). He is equally present in his word since it is he who speaks when the holy Scriptures are read in the church.
>
> As for the eucharistic sacrifice, he is present there and in the person of the minister, for "it is the same [sacrifice] that is offered now through the ministry of the priest as he offered himself on the cross,"[1] and, above all, in the eucharistic species. In this sacrament, indeed, Christ is present in a

1. Council of Trent, Session XXIII, Decree on the Mass, chapter II, Denz. 940.

unique way, whole and entire, God and man, substantially and permanently. This presence of Christ in the species is called "real," not because it is the only one (as if the others were not real) but by reason of its excellence.

4. Assembly in the Reformed Churches, Importance of the
(see pp. 50 and 144)

It was in the name of the Gospel that Luther, Calvin, Zwingli and Farel stood up against Low Masses where "the priest alone offers a sacrifice," against the "meritorious" and clerical function of the cantor representing the community of the laity, and against the absence of preaching of the Gospel at Mass. They affirmed that there was no worship of God without an assembly, since worship is the epiphany of the church where Christ himself is present, in the preached word of the Gospel which actualizes the great deeds of God, and in "the sacrament of the altar." The only sacrifice that believers can offer is the sacrifice of praise, expressing a joy that no words can express, springing from the gift received in faith through hearing the word in the Gospel. This response must be something that every believer does; through prayer and singing inspired by the Holy Spirit, believers manifest brotherly/sisterly love among themselves and bear witness to the world of the salvation accomplished in Jesus Christ. This response of believers to God's gift in Jesus Christ, this expression of love of neighbor, this proclamation to the world—all this makes use of vernacular language: the mystery of salvation is to be found in the midst of the everyday. Worship was thus a first area of priority for the Reformation: reforms in catechesis, ecclesiastical discipline and structures all sprang from worship and are to some extent modeled on worship. Indeed, the community gathered around Jesus Christ does not express how little or how great is its religiosity but acknowledges how much or how little is its faithfulness to its Lord. The community is the battlefield where the tempter sets his traps and his trials. How can the community emerge victorious from this ordeal? Its praise is always a response to the gift of God received in faith. It is united to the heavenly worship of the angels, prophets, apostles, and martyrs, and the tempter seeks in vain to put asunder what God has joined together in the jubilation of a Spirit which demands to "be made incarnate" in the liturgical singing of all. Not everyone can themselves choose the words and the music to express their praise: this choice is left to poets and musicians who are qualified and recognized by the church.

The assembly and the choir (of young boys or young girls) and the organ can intervene by turns. The organ sustains the singing of the assembly and the singing of the choir, or it sustains instruments if there are any. The absence of the choir is regrettable, but it never means that the assembly is therefore silent. Luther ascribed to liturgical singing the quality of "*cooperatio praedicandi*" (co-operating in preaching the word) under the action of the Holy Spirit. This affirmation asks for explanations, but in any case it means that reformed worship is not merely the preaching of the word: the liturgical response of the assembly is an integral part of the worship.

5. Beauty and Suitability (see pp. 44, 86, and 161)

How do we make a value judgment on the quality of a musical action within the liturgical action? According to musical principles or liturgical principles? Neither one nor the other, but very precisely according to both. It will be useful for us to review the notions which have kept the church alive over the centuries, and, moreover, well before and for much longer than the recent and ambiguous notion of "sacred music" (see GL 46, p. 159).

St. Augustine, in a treatise which has unfortunately been lost but to which he makes reference and on which he expands in his Confessions, distinguished the aesthetic of the beautiful (the *pulchrum*) from the aesthetic of the suitable (the *aptum*: something suitable for or apt for . . .).

"I took notice, and I saw in these bodies two aspects: it was one thing to be whole, as it were, and therefore beautiful, and quite another thing for something to be attractive because aptly suited to something else, like a part of the body to the whole, the shoe to the foot, and other similar cases. And this consideration began to well up in my mind from the depths of my heart, and I wrote some books *De Pulchro et Apto* ('On the Beautiful and the Fitting'), two or three, I think—you know, O God, for the details have escaped me. Indeed, we no longer have these books, but they have strayed far away from us, I know not how." (Confessions, IV, XIII, 20)

Henri Davenson (whose real name is actually Henri Marrou) commented on this in his *Traité de la musique selon saint Augustin*:

"Beauty is what pleases by itself; it is opposed to the other type of perfection, that of an object or an act drawing its value from having been adapted in order to achieve a certain result distinct from itself."[2] St. Augustine makes the point, when talking about the shoe, that it is not sufficient for the shoe to be beautiful: it must also fit properly.

This is precisely the quality that we look for in music in the liturgy: not only must the music be beautiful, but its "type of perfection" must be suited both to the ritual moment where it occurs or is sung and to the actors who use it in the rite. Thus we can grasp how much Vatican II, while still keeping the term "sacred music," returned to St. Augustine's traditional distinctions in order to define the term. "Sacred music will be the more holy the more closely it is linked with the liturgical action" (*Sacrosanctum Concilium*, no. 112).

6. Bells, Large and Small (see p. 76)

Large bells and handbells were known to nearly all primitive peoples who used them for many different purposes. They passed easily into monastic usage, and thence into parochial usage. Abbots had no difficulty in finding a way to bring religious together for the various hours of the office: they simply adopted the methods of fishmongers for attracting the attention of customers, of the "bath boys" for announcing the opening of the thermal baths ... There was probably little uniformity about all this: here you would find a little bell, there a large gong, elsewhere a bronze bowl or a set of jingles—it didn't much matter. Gradually the use of a handbell spread, and then of a suspended bell operated by a rope, passing from monasteries into parish churches. Celtic lands preserved the bells of a number of saints (including St. Patrick) as precious relics.[3] In the sixth century the use of bells became the norm in Gaul. At first their role was to alert the faithful that it was time to gather in the church, but bells were also used to solemnize certain moments in the Mass (the elevation, the *Gloria* on Holy Thursday and at the Easter Vigil),

---

2. Editions de la Baconnière, 1942, p. 16.

3. The Irish word for bell is *clog*, from which we get (eventually) the English "clock" and the French *cloche* (bell).

moments during the day (the *Angelus*), certain days (the vigils of great feasts), certain events in the life of the parish (baptism, confirmation, marriage, viaticum, death agony, death itself, funerals, pastoral visit of the bishop) or in the life of the church, but also events taking place in the community (fire, storm, hailstorms) or the nation (war, victory . . .).

7. Cantillation (see pp. 37 and 97)

The first meaning of the Latin *cantillare* is "to hum a tune." Nevertheless, in liturgical music the word refers to a very precise vocal act. The term was invented by modern musicology to characterize recitatives in Judaeo-Christian worship. In fact it designates a way of singing a text that is close to the recitative of religious cantatas. In keeping to a single note, cantillation remains as faithful as possible to the text. However, it can emphasize the articulations of the text by the introduction of formulas, e.g., incipit, flex, mediant, cadence. It is therefore a way of declaiming a text: biblical reading, prayer, preface of the eucharistic prayer, dialogue between minister and assembly.

8. Centonization (see p. 97)

The Latin *cento* (Greek *kentrôn*) means a covering or a costume made up of little pieces of cloth of many colors—in fact a harlequin outfit. An author centonizes when she or he produces a text through a patchwork of citations drawn from many different famous works. In the same way, a musician can be said to centonize when she or he sets out to re-use many different melodies within a single "new" composition. This process is frequently found in Gregorian chant where certain formulas (intonation, *jubilus*, links, and cadences) have undergone multiple re-usages. It even occurs when recent Latin liturgical texts are set to music (e.g., plainchant Masses for feasts that have recently been inserted into the calendar of the Roman rite).

Centonization has also been subject to a quasi-humorous monodic development in folksong (for example, different potpourris), and to a different kind of development that is both serious and full of humor in the field of polyphony (in Germany, Flanders, and Burgundy, for example).

9. Church and Music, The (see p. 102)

It was only very late that the Roman Church took action in codifying its ritual practice concerning music. In the early centuries—and it is still generally the case today in the Eastern Churches—what was recognized as good was recognized as the law. Ultimate interventions came from authorities reacting against occasional abuses.

When the Fathers of the church warned against the dangers of lascivious songs or pagan forms of music, they were primarily talking about social life rather than Christian worship. It was from the sixth century onward, when the role of psalmists and cantors was developing, that certain voices (e.g., St. Gregory the Great and Pseudo-Pambo) were raised against ways of singing that were too worldly or too theatrical. For Isidore of Seville (who would inspire the whole of the Middle Ages on this subject), ecclesiastical singing had to possess the characteristics of simplicity, decency, and also charm (*De Eccl. Off.*, 2, 12).

The first papal intervention as such came in the fourteenth century with John XXII. In the face of the sometimes intemperate polyphonic experiments of *Ars nova*, he called the church back to a respect for the melody and text of the traditional Gregorian chant. Speaking at a time when polyphonic art had reached its summit, the Council of Trent asked only that the words remain distinguishable; but it also reacted against the entry into the sanctuary of any kind of music in which "is mixed something of the lascivious or the impure" (Sess. XXII).

In the following centuries, the church battled more and more sternly against the invasion of the "operatic" style into liturgical compositions, starting with Benedict XIV (*Annus Qui*, 1749) and ending with St. Pius X (*Tra le sollecitudini*, 1903). The 1917 Code of Canon Law (1264, par. 1) took up Trent's theme again and urged observance of the liturgical rules concerning music.

By the time of Pius XII, it was felt that the situation was evolving; but we had to wait until the Second Vatican Council for a full and perceptive treatment of, on the one hand, the relationship of music to the rite, and, on the other hand, the relationship of music to the surrounding culture.

10. Culture (see p. 41)

Obviously we are using the word culture here in its broadest sense, as encompassing everything that allows a people to define itself, to recognize itself, to discover what it calls "its identity." This concept integrates all forms of tradition, language, customs, dress, artistic and craft forms, ways of life, social structure, etc. Like the concept of art, the notion of culture has for a number of years been undergoing a rejuvenating process, in the course of which it has emerged from within the iron yoke of a previous restrictive and elitist concept wherein culture was equated with erudition and knowledge.

11. Eucharist (see p. 67)

In Greek, *eucharistia* means thanksgiving.

By this word Christians intend first of all to signify that deep dimension which traverses all human existence: the act of giving thanks. By the Spirit, following Christ, humanity sees itself called to offer its life to the Father; to give back to the Father its life enriched with all the work of the physical dimension, to render to God a thankfulness charged with the authentic weight of incarnation.

The liturgy thus becomes the *locus* where this essential movement in human existence is able to express itself in a way that is simultaneously symbolic, efficacious, and prophetic. The Mass, just as simply called "eucharist," allows the assembly to make memorial of the sacrifice that Christ offered as perfect praise to the Father (anamnetic dimension) and to call on the Spirit to make the assembly become in its turn "a living sacrifice of praise to his glory" (epicletic dimension) as one of the Roman eucharistic prayers states it. These two dimensions, anamnesis and epiclesis, "organize" the great prayer which follows the liturgy of the word and which we call "eucharistic prayer." This prayer can most surely be traced back to the action accomplished by Jesus at his Last Supper with his disciples; and this action is in its turn rooted in the Jewish liturgical tradition.

From its origins up to the present, the celebration of the eucharist has remained the same in its basic structure. Depending on regions, eras, and equally on the whim of poetic and artistic sensitivity, the forms of the eucharist have known a legitimate diversity. The wide range of liturgical families has thus contributed to enriching and making incarnate the prayer of thanksgiving until the Savior comes again. But this wide range encompasses many different ways of expressing the same basic schema: thanksgiving, *Sanctus* acclamation, epiclesis over the gifts, institution narrative, anamnesis, offering, epiclesis over the communicants, intercessions, doxology.

12. Festivity (see p. 63)

The notion of festivity is one of the richest in human values. Normally people are taken up with their work, their worries, their cares. They do not have time. They therefore feel an intense desire to take time out, devoting it to what is important for them: their family, their country, their personal history, their faith . . .

From this desire grows every kind of festivity, which will accordingly be a time in one's life destined to be occupied with "what is deepest in our hearts." Thus New Year's Day is a feastday of life, July 4th (in the United States) is a feastday of nationhood, Easter is a feastday of the Risen Christ on which our faith is founded. In addition, my birthday is a feastday in my personal history . . . and then there is Mothers' Day, golden wedding anniversaries, baptisms . . . Festivity is first and foremost a consecration of time to something that is essential.

To achieve its goal, festivity breaks with the everyday. Normally we are trying to save money, we are in a hurry, we are serious . . . For merrymaking we spend money (on food, clothes), we take time (linger at table or go for a walk), we have fun (play, put on fancy dress, tell jokes) . . . To express the importance of what is being celebrated, not much is needed in the way of words, which is why festivity uses symbols (see GL 54, p. 167). Saying "I love you" to your mother is over very quickly; a gift says it more strongly and lasts longer. Saying how happy you are is fine, but fireworks or candles or music for dancing help to prove it more strongly, since we are not just saying it but living it.

At the end of the day, festivity is the great moment in the life of society. It is even for "being together" that festivity exists. It is not just a notion that we need to set aside time. It is not of high ideas that we are deprived, it is of all those beings which are dear to us. If a man organizes festivities, it is to have more time with his wife and children, to have all his family around him once again, to renew acquaintances and friendships, to be in communion with all the inhabitants of his village or his country.

One of the best ways of doing this is a banquet. In the course of the banquet we eat and drink more than usual. But we also talk and sing and make speeches. This signifies at a deep level that, far from being content with eating this dish or drinking this wine, we are "drinking in" the words of those who are dear to us, and we "eat our fill" of their presence with us. As well as their physical bodies, people need to nourish their "social bodies."

So we can understand why music and singing, which are so strongly symbolic of communion (see GL 54, p. 167 and GL 58, p. 170), have such an important place in every kind of festivity.

13. Festivity and Music (see p. 86)

There can be no festivity without music, which is: deployment of freely-given energies and elements of playfulness; "aestheticization" of space, time, action; amplification, emphasizing, solemnization of the voice and the word. We need to look carefully at the corresponding demands since the opposite statement ("There can be no music without festivity") is certainly not true.

14. Fine Arts (see p. 34)

If the *technè* of the Greeks and the *ars* of the Romans encompassed everything which today we would include under the headings of "knowledge," "art," and "*savoir-faire*," our modern age has seen the growth and development of an opposition between artist and artisan, the first tending towards an aesthetic and decorative creativity, the second aiming at the production of useful artifacts. The notion of "fine arts" has simply served to underline this aesthetic dimension, just like the concept of "serious music" which is often used today. In this kind of terminology we can see not only the desire to distinguish between two ends but also to set up a hierarchy and an order of ranking in value (great art, serious music, "minor" arts . . .). This corresponds to the idea of artists "inspired" by the Muses, almost effortlessly finding the source of their work within their own imagination.

The twentieth century is gradually recovering a more realistic concept of artistic activity, accentuating the "action" aspect of creativity. Liturgico-musical activity (and isn't the liturgy itself etymologically also an action?) comes close to this modern notion of art; and it is certainly a fortunate opening which will allow composers and performers to aim less at the work—the repertoire to be created and re-created—and rather more at the musical action integrated into the totality of the liturgical action.

15. Function of Music (see p. 59)

Before one determines the function of music in ritual, an examination of the function of music must be made. Edward Foley in *Music in Ritual: A Pre-Theological Investigation* (originally published in 1984 by The Pastoral Press, but now available from The Liturgical Press) suggests that music has four functions which various people have claimed as the reason why music is used in ritual: music as powerful; music as communication; music as language; and music as symbol. Historically, empirically, and experientially, music is understood to be a powerful phenomenon. In an effort to explain the "power," music is often understood in terms of communication. The communication designation, Foley concludes, does not seem to go far enough in explaining how music mediates any message or in pinpointing how music unleashes power. Because of music's incapacity for fixed meanings, syntax, or grammar, music's linguistic nature could not be maintained as its reason for use in the liturgy. Foley concludes that the presentational symbolic activity is the most appropriate designation for defining and understanding music's powerful capacity for mediating any message.

Michael Joncas (*Worship*, May 1992), in analyzing the position of *Musicam Sacram* in section 5, concludes that there are five functions of music: alluring or decorative, differentiating, unifying, transcendental, and eschatological.

The alluring or decorative function asserts that singing "gives a more graceful expression to prayer." The differentiating function asserts that singing "brings out more distinctly the hierarchic character of the liturgy and the specific make-up of the community." The unifying function stresses that musical liturgy "achieves a closer union of hearts through the union of voices." The transcendental function states that musical worship "raises the mind more readily to heavenly realities through the splendor of the rites." Finally, the eschatological function points out that music "makes the whole celebration a more striking symbol of the celebration to come in the heavenly Jerusalem."

16. Function to Mission: An Open Constraint (see p. 91)

Some musicians and music-lovers fall into the temptation of believing that liturgical music is less "musical" than other forms because liturgical music is at the service of the rite. It is true that certain unfortunate examples would lead one to think that this was the case. But it is precisely because these examples are unfortunate that we have the right to maintain (and we are glad to say) that they do not exhaust all that music is capable of in liturgy.

Music designed for the rite is no less music than any other kind. In fact, by being music for the rite, it is also music for music—in other words, music for everything that music produces in human beings.

It is true that musical action in the liturgy is constrained action:

• constrained by the ritual: we do not do anything we like whenever we feel like it (an entrance chant is not a penitential invocation, and a post-Vatican II penitential preparatory rite is not a *Kyrie* from the Mass of the era of St. Pius V);

• constrained by practice: we do not do what we do with just anyone and anywhere (a little country parish is not a cathedral).

For a particular kind of music to be suitable for the liturgy, we will never skimp on the ritual function that this music has to fulfill, nor on the practical situation into which it has to be integrated. But musical art in liturgy is not exhausted in its conception of function. From the very moment when music is made in such a way that it is well suited to its function (we tend to say that "it fits well" rather than "it is suitable," or perhaps even that "it is congruous"— which is exactly what it must be: a congruent part), from that very moment can be born what the Ancients called *delectatio*—the "pleasure," even the joy, produced by a moment of grace.

We could say that this is something unusual for music. Here we have a kind of music which is not made out of anything other than itself but which is equally the product of the action which fixes the music's norms, the product of the actors who use the music to attain something (or Someone) other than the music itself, and the product of the place and time which impose their own conditions on it ... Here we have a kind of music which seems to be in a state of servitude but which in reality penetrates everything with its vibrations and reveals that, far from being a slave of the rite, it actually becomes the soul of the rite ... Here we have a kind of music which is generous enough to accept a role of service and then freely offers all its potential, up to the point where it transforms into music what was not music at the outset: the liturgical action, with whose mechanism it integrates itself in order to lead the liturgical actors far beyond themselves towards the effects of symbol and of the imagination that it bears within itself; the liturgical time that it gives rhythm to, and the liturgical seasons that it binds together; the stones, the stained glass, the different kinds of light that it gives life to, making them appear to sing ...

Whereas a concert aims to reduce as far as possible the distance separating transmission from reception (the greatest reduction is obtained by solitary listening through headphones), the liturgy asks music to open the believer up to the largest possible gathering: a gathering-together of the body and soul of each participant; a gathering-together of each person with the other members of the community and, through them, the members of the Universal Community; a gathering-together of the entire cosmos summed up in a single place; a gathering-together of all the living in the heavens and on the earth; and lastly a gathering-together with God.

Where else is music called to such a work of formation? Where else is music given such power, such a mission?

17. Functions and Practices (see p. 86)

The *Universa Laus* group has over the course of twenty years developed an essentially original theoretical process of reflection based on the "anthropological functions" of music. This process has also been nourished by musicological studies (from Combarieu to Blacking) and linguistic studies (see GL 23, p. 131). So it is within this "tradition" that we find the best context for deepening our understanding of the terms used by the document. However, two general remarks will prove useful.

First, each function is only realized for certain aspects of music and under certain conditions: therefore it is necessary to pursue the analysis to this concrete point; otherwise a general statement on a function runs the risk of being empty or even false.

Second, the functions mentioned can be in the realm of physical effects, or material effects, or effects of direction or meaning. Normally the two aspects go together, especially in celebration where all technique becomes a symbol by the very fact of its existence. Nevertheless the document indicates the cases where it is good to distinguish between the two.

18. Heart, The (see p. 72)

According to Scripture the heart is not first of all linked to the emotional life. A person's heart is what is inside: the interior as opposed to what is outside. The heart is the opposite of appearances: "Humans look at appearances, whereas God looks at the heart" (1 Sm 16:7).

The heart is where thought is to be found:

> O search me, God, and know my heart;
> O test me and know my thoughts.
>   (Ps 138:23)

The heart is a place of openness and of closedness:

> O that today you would listen to his voice!
> Harden not your heart . . .
>   (Ps 94:7-8)

The heart is the potential place for sin:

> They speak words of peace to their neighbors
> but with evil in their hearts.
>   (Ps 27: 3)

And the heart is also the place of forgiveness, of forgiveness received from God:

> A pure heart create for me, O God,
> put a steadfast spirit within me.
>   (Ps 50:12)

The heart is also the place of a forgiveness which burns and which brings understanding: "Did not our hearts burn within us as he spoke to us on the road and opened the Scriptures to us?" (Lk

24:32) and the place of pardon given to our brethren: "Be good to one another, forgive each other from your hearts" (Eph 4:32). In Xavier Leon-Dufour's *Dictionary of Biblical Theology* we read: "The heart is the place where humankind meets with God, an encounter which has its effect in the human heart of the Son of God."

19. Humming (see p. 75)

A vocal technique used to produce a particular effect in the performance of a chant. For example, the choir, or part of it, may hum as it repeats a passage that has just been sung (e.g., a verse or a refrain). This process allows the same music to come to life in a different way, and the technique is frequently encountered in the accompaniment of singing by a soloist (or a unison group of equal voices), the other voices creating the harmony.

20. "Indeterminable Functions" (see p. 81)

Every piece of liturgical music has one or more functions that are determined and desired by those who have drawn up the musical program of the celebration: for example, the entrance song's function is to build up the assembly and to introduce the celebration which follows. But because music is art and therefore acts on people's sensibilities, it exercises far more than functions that can be determined from outside. One could even go so far as to say that music acts without the knowledge of the listeners or participants and touches their unconscious. Musical animators do well to convince themselves of the reality of this "indeterminable" action so that they accept that music can have other effects than the one they themselves had foreseen, and that their animating role has its limits. Here we are talking about a "professional" requirement as much as we are about spiritual humility.

21. Kingdom, The (see pp. 36 and 107)

Every Christian who prays like Jesus has learned to ask for the coming of the Kingdom: "Your Kingdom come!"—the Heavenly Kingdom and the Kingdom of God are equivalent expressions. They spring up throughout the Gospel. The announcement of the Kingdom opens Christ's public life: "The Kingdom of God is at hand" (Mt 3:2). A further reminder closes his life in the midst of his own, at the Last Supper, before he undergoes his Passion: "I shall not drink of this fruit of the vine again until I drink the new wine with you in the Kingdom of my Father" (Mt 26:29). And when he evokes the Last Judgment, Jesus tells us that the King says "Come, you blessed of my Father, inherit the Kingdom prepared for you since the foundation of the world" (Mt 25:34).

This reality is not easy to discern; it is always in the course of coming to be. Only Jesus knows it, and he reveals it only to the humble and to children (Mt 11:25) by using the images of the parables: the wedding feast, the harvest, the mustard seed, the pearl of great price, the division into sheep and goats, the talents and the day of reckoning. This Kingdom spoken of by Jesus is in a direct line of succession to the Kingdom of God in the psalms: "Proclaim to the nations: God is King" (Ps 95:10). The God-King of the psalter reigns in justice, righteousness, and truth, for the happiness of his people and the gathering of all the peoples, for the defense of the poor, the oppressed, the foreigners. Jesus does the same: he gives the Beatitudes as the charter of his Kingdom; he refuses to be the king dreamed of by his contemporaries; he receives this title only when he is humiliated before Pilate (Jn 18:37); he only accepts the scroll on the throne of the Cross (Jn 19:21). It is the Kingdom of this King (whose "coming in glory we await") which the liturgy announces, celebrates, calls us to, and builds up.

22. Knowledge and Sensibility[4] (see p. 65)

Our civilization has separated what can be perceived by the intelligence from what can be perceived by the senses. It places knowledge in the realm of the intellect, and sensibility in the realm of the senses and the emotions. In a balanced and unified human being, knowledge will be sufficiently incarnated to become sensed

---

4. The text is easier to understand when it is realized that, in French, the words *savoir* and *saveur* (translated here as "knowledge" and "sensibility"—but literally "know-how"—and "savor" or "taste") have the same etymological root. The text also plays with the difference between, for example, *savoir* and *connaissance*, and between *sensibilité* and *affectivité*, distinctions difficult to render satisfactorily into English - translator's note.

in all the fibers of that person's being, and sensibility will also take its place in the area of the understanding.

Through the use of the vernacular language the liturgical reform gave pride of place to the understanding, the intelligibility of texts. We still have the task of rediscovering the "sense" dimension of the liturgical act so that our entire being might participate in praise. Art in all its forms, the person and a person's component parts—body, spirit and heart—and recourse to silence will all contribute to creating this total dimension within a liturgy that is overburdened with ideas and words. Wisdom (*sapientia*) will then encompass both knowledge and sensibility . . .

23. Language, Functions of (see pp. 68 and 127)

It is up to a "celebratory" or liturgical "competence" to refine its sensitivity as much as possible to the deep riches of human language. The document explicitly asks for this when it makes reference to "functions of language" in terms which are immediately clear to all but which can make their point even more strongly if we root them in the context of contemporary linguistics. In a practical and summary way, we can say that the ultimate purpose of language is to communicate (Martinet). But an analysis of the different components of communication (transmitter, receiver, contact, referent, message, channel) already suggests a lattice of corresponding functions (expressive, conative, phatic, referential, poetic, metalinguistic) (Jakobson). On the other hand, a theory of the "acts of language" (Austin, Searle) underlines the different "modalities of speech" (Greimas) (doing, doing-being, having someone do something, telling) that can be reformulated as functions of allocution, interpretation, persuasion, etc. Finally, in digging deeper into "communicative competence" (Eymes, Halliday), we can on the one hand reach the stage of nominating other projects realizable by human beings and groupings in the language and, on the other hand, reach the stage of seeing the language itself tangled up in a very complex network of cognitive and emotive structures and modes of behavior. This is why the terms used by the document, in talking about the "functions of language," deliberately steer clear of any particular theoretical table, and instead refer to an anthropological level where for the purposes of celebration technique and symbol can and must join their individual strands together.

24. Latin in the Liturgy (see p. 43)

It was natural for the earliest Christian communities to adopt for their liturgy the language that they spoke: Aramaic in the Judaeo-Christian Churches, Greek throughout the Mediterranean basin, and Latin in Roman Africa. The first testimonies to the liturgy in Rome were in Greek (the Apostolic Tradition of Hippolytus). Latin was adopted in Rome in the fourth century when it had become the common language. Subsequently, whereas the Eastern Churches retained the custom of using in the liturgy the language of the country, the west remained attached to Latin, the language of culture, understood only by clerics, but the only language (it was thought) capable of correctly expressing the Christian mysteries and maintaining unity in the face of a flood of barbarian languages. The liturgy, in its verbal expression, remained foreign to the people; but the faithful participated in other ways: hymns, processions, listening to Latin chants . . . In the context of a mentality which had a horror of change, Latin was received as a "given" handed down by tradition; we were firmly attached to it, and its exclusive use in the west was justified by the inscription on the cross: in Hebrew, in Greek, and in Latin. The demands of the Reformers for an intelligible language for worship were too closely associated with their "errors" not to be completely rejected by the Council of Trent. In 1670 the Jesuits introduced Mass in Chinese into China; it was banned in 1755—European spirits were not ready for it. During the French Revolution attempts to have liturgy in French in the constitutional Church provoked disapproval from the faithful. Even the simple translation of the Latin texts of the liturgy was suspect, and the missal was not translated into French till 1897.[5] In 1903 St. Pius X's

---

5. From early in the nineteenth century, translations of the missal and even the the breviary had appeared in English (in spite of Pope Alexander VII's prohibition in the seventeenth century), and possibly much earlier; but these were mostly beyond the financial reach of ordinary lay people. A bilingual Order of Mass and the epistles and gospels in English had appeared in nineteenth-century editions of the devotional work *The Garden of the Soul*, but the first popular (and affordable) English version of the full Roman Missal—it also gave the propers, the Ordinary and the Canon in Latin—did not appear until 1915 (produced by the distinguished liturgist Adrian Fortescue). This was followed by others translated from French (by Cabrol) and later Belgian (Monastery of St-André) sources.

motu proprio on sacred music was still forbidding the use of vernacular languages in the liturgy. The church had to wait till the middle of the twentieth century to see the gradual introduction of living languages, starting with the sacramental rites: in France, a bilingual ritual in 1947 and a similar publication in English in the early 1950s (although only the Latin text was used in celebration). Vatican II's Liturgy Constitution (1963) recognized Latin as the language proper to the Roman Church, but opened up the liturgy to diverse tongues. Fifteen years later, it was possible to observe that the Roman liturgy was being celebrated in 342 languages.

25. Liturgical Action, Music Integrated into (see p. 93)

Liturgy is an action, as is clear if we consider the etymology of the word itself. The "urgy" of liturgy—from the Greek *ergon,* meaning work, action, function—is the same as in metallurgy and in (with a little corruption in the form of the word) surgery. The difference is that it is not work done with the hand (surgery) or with metal; rather, it is the work of the people: the Greek *leitos,* which is the root of the "lit" in liturgy, is an adjectival form of the Greek *laos,* which means "people." Liturgy is therefore an action of people, a public function.

For reasons which derive from the nature of those social beings whom we call humans, it so happens that from the very beginning of its history (and St. Paul witnesses to this, e.g., in Colossians 3:16) the church has used music, and particularly singing, in its celebrations; moreover, the church has never stopped doing so. In a liturgy which is totally an action, how could music then be anything else but a musical action?

There is "absolute production" where, in a concert for instance, the only goal of the musicians is to make music; and there is "absolute listening" where the listeners, whether at a concert or by means of the radio or a sound-system, have as their only goal to be led toward the music itself. But music in the liturgy, on the contrary, always leads toward something other than itself. The musical action is integrated into the liturgical action in order to be an integrating factor in its turn: it must facilitate the participants' entering into what the liturgy is asking them to do (which is always something other than making music, even if music is the means to this end). Whatever pleasure a believer may take in listening to a vocal or instrumental piece in a celebration, or in singing a song for the assembly, these pieces or songs are not there just for the believer's pleasure but to allow praise or petition to assume a form—one might even say, to assume a bodily form.

Lastly, music in liturgy always remains in the realm of music, but it is transfigured.

26. Liturgy in the Roman Church, Unification of (see p. 42)

The history of the liturgy in the west is a constant alternating motion between decentralization and centralization that extends over long periods of time. In Christian antiquity the liturgy was celebrated according to the usage of the local church, and thus enjoyed a wide diversity of customs. The liturgical differences between Rome, Milan, Lyon, and Carthage were not causes for astonishment: rather, they appeared as a source of enrichment for the unity of the church. The authenticity of the liturgy was assured by the local bishop within a given framework: the deposit of faith received from the tradition of the apostles.

Controversies on delicate points such as the date of Easter, the preponderant influence of sees established in important towns of the Empire, and the meetings of provincial councils—all brought in their train a movement toward unification by each province. But from the second century onward, the bishop of Rome affirmed his "divine" right to legislate for the liturgy of the entire church. The missionaries sent by Rome to England and Germany introduced Roman books and customs in these countries.

However, it was not the Roman See but civil authority (Pepin, Charlemagne) which undertook, for political reasons, the work of liturgical unification in the Western Empire: there was to be only one rite just as there was one law, one pope just as there was one emperor. However, this unification managed to accommodate diverse and even divergent local customs right through the Middle Ages.

The liturgical reform which followed the Council of Trent (the so-called "St Pius V" Missal and Breviary) sought to bring the prayer of the church back to ancient tradition and to uniformity in the rules for celebration. This desire for unity was tempered with flexibility: churches possessing "proper" books and usages for at least two hundred years previously were invited to keep them. General usage remained diversified by custom. However, the popes gradually withdrew from the local bishops the power that these bishops had till then exercised. The bishops themselves, often against the will of their chapter, undertook to impose Roman books and usages. In spite of this, the Congregation of Rites (established in 1588) persisted in deciding on the smallest details in order to obtain a total uniformity (4,404 decrees passed up to 1926).

In the eighteenth century, especially but not solely in France, there were efforts at a liturgical renewal, even though Rome was clinging strictly to a *status quo*. Each diocese had its own proper missal and breviary; there was a kind of anarchy abroad. After the post-Revolution period with its redrawing of the map of the dioceses, Napoleon tried to impose the Parisian liturgy which had already taken over more than half the French dioceses; but his plan did not come to fruition. His place was taken by Dom Guéranger, whose project was to re-establish the Roman liturgy in France. At first the Holy See was reluctant to do so, but subsequently it approved and encouraged this idea, finally forcing the bishops' hands without taking into account the suffering that would be caused. In the end, unification was accomplished between 1840 and 1875. The bishops now were no more than custodians of a liturgy which had been codified outside their sphere of influence.

The modern discipline of centralization at its climax is precisely summed up in the 1917 Code of Canon Law: "To the Holy See alone belongs the right to organize or approve the liturgical books" (Canon 1257); and similarly in the encyclical *Mediator Dei* of 1947: "To the Sovereign Pontiff alone belongs the right to recognize and establish all usage concerning divine worship, to introduce and approve new rites, and to modify those which he judges should be changed" (no. 58).

The 1963 Constitution on the Liturgy opened up the way toward a new movement of decentralization: "The regulation of the liturgy depends solely on the authority of the church, that is, on the Apostolic See and, accordingly as the law determines, on the bishop" (no. 22). Here it is not a question of returning to the liturgical freedom in force before Trent, and certainly not in our age when distances are seen to become smaller and feelings of community solidarity are seen to become larger. But the proper authority of the local bishop is reaffirmed, defined, and enhanced; it is acknowledged that a proper power of decision belongs to national bishops' conferences.

The implementation of these principles has led in the course of twenty years to the double motion that we have already seen throughout liturgical history, but here it is happening simultaneously. The liturgy is becoming decentralized, makes use of vernacular languages, and is striving for adaptation and inculturation, but under the authority of episcopal conferences and the Holy See (see Constitution on the Liturgy, nos. 37 and 40).

27. Liturgy of the Hours (see p. 67)

Christ is the alpha and the omega of all creation: human time therefore belongs to him—time measured out during the year, the week, the day, which in the liturgy becomes time sanctified by the prayer of the church. Following the example of the Jews, who gave a rhythm to the day by moments of prayer in common, the first Christians also showed themselves to be practitioners of a form of prayer which, based on the Roman division of the day, soon assumed a large hierarchical and symbolic structure.

At the beginning of the Middle Ages, the monastic *cursus* exercised a determinative influence on the organization of prayer in communities. There was the creation and development of certain hours and of euchological elements (antiphons, responsories, hymns, readings, homiletic or hagiographic commentaries, intercessions). The liturgical reform of Vatican II, making use not only of traditions but of the previous radical reforms (e.g., the Breviary of the Curia toward the end of the Middle Ages, reforms of Pius V and Pius IX), is evidence of an attempt to restore the prayer of the hours to all the people. Praise of the Father was to become the *opus* of everyone.

Daily Cursus of the Liturgy of the Hours

Before Vatican II	After Vatican II
• Matins	• Office of Readings
• Lauds	• Morning Prayer
• Prime	
• Terce	
• Sext	• Midday Prayer (or Terce-Sext-None
• None	if all three are required)
• Vespers	• Evening Prayer
• Compline	• Night Prayer

28. "Media Vita" Responsory, The (see p. 96)

This responsory was formerly attributed, falsely so, to Notker (d. 912), but is more likely the work of an anonymous eleventh-century composer. It does not belong to the monastic *cursus* but to the Roman *cursus*. Hartker's Antiphonary does not contain it, but we find it in the Bamberg Antiphonary (Codex lit. 23—end of the eleventh century) and in the Verona Antiphonary (Codex 98—twelfth century).

Its liturgical usage is varied. Bamberg has it at lauds on Holy Saturday, while in Verona it is found at compline as an antiphon to the *Nunc dimittis*. It could be used on the Saturday after the 3rd Sunday in Lent—in certain parts of England it was used from the 3rd Sunday of Lent up to Passion Sunday. At Tours it was sung on the last day of the year. Sometimes we find it used as a responsory following every verse of the *Nunc dimittis*.

This responsory, appearing in the Dominican liturgy, moved St. Thomas Aquinas most profoundly (according to William of Tocco). We find it in the Carmelite ordinary in 1312, in the Roman processional of the male and female religious of the order of St. Francis for use in times of plague, and in the monastic processionals of the Norbertines and Benedictines "*ad usum congregationis Galliae*" ("for the use of the French province") in 1393.

The number of verses found with the responsory varies—sometimes there are as many as six.

A curious phenomenon is the way in which the use of this responsory passed into the paraliturgical domain and even into the civil domain. Thus it was used as a prayer of supplication in times of public calamity, such as in Liège in the second half of the thirteenth century after torrential rains. On this occasion it was followed by the *Salve regina*. The Wurtemberg missal of 1484 gives it as "*pro vitanda mortalitate et tempore pestilentiae*" ("for avoidance of death and in time of pestilence"). In May 1294 the clergy of Bremen sang it as they celebrated a crusade victory over the pagans.

It came to be used as a form of violent protest against abuses of power by authorities. In 1255 the Duke of Brabant had a difference of opinion with the chapter of St. Lambert in Liège, which "sang" the *Media vita* at him. The same thing happened to a prince-bishop who refused to withdraw counterfeit coinage . . .

At Trier in the thirteenth century, a landed gentleman from Malberg was persecuting the nuns of St. Thomas-an-der-Kyll; as a result, the nuns processed every day into the cathedral singing the *Lamentabiliter* from the *Media vita* responsory. In 1263 Archbishop Henri violated the rights of free election of the monks of St. Mathias, so they prostrated themselves on the ground and "sang" for him the *Media vita* in a style described as "*lacrimabiliter*."

In the face of such abuses, since by this time miraculous powers were being attributed to the chant, the Synod of Cologne in 1390 forbade its use without the express permission of the archbishop. However, this did not stop it from being sung. The Canonesses Regular of Wennigen (Hanover) refused to accept the reforms that were being imposed on them and so threw themselves to the ground while singing the chant. In 1455 the Cistercians of Mariense threw lighted candles at the reformers to the accompaniment of the *Media vita* chant. One young monk went so far as to bite the ground and throw stones . . .

Early on, the chant was "farced."

Luther made an adaptation of it in his chorale *Mitten wir im Leben sind*. In the nineteenth century at the monastery of Beuron and also in Belgium, this chant was sung to celebrate golden jubilees of religious life. (See *Revue liturgique et monastique*, vol. 2, 1926, pp. 125-128-188 on "The Antiphon *Media vita* in the Middle Ages" by U. Berlière O.S.B., and P. Wagner's "The *Media vita*" in Schweizer's *Jahrbuch für Musikwissenschaft*, 1924, pp. 18-40.)

29. Music Creating a Gulf (see p. 63)

Certain types of music calm and soothe us. When singing is involved, these run the risk of watering down the text they are carrying. How many melodies have toned down, even to the point of having us forget, the vigorous and unsettling character of the *Magnificat*.

The other side of the coin is that there are kinds of music that awaken us, that surprise and shock us. Through the use of strange timbres, unexpected rhythms, weird scales and melodic constructions, and particularly bizarre harmonies, certain types of music can create a feeling of dislocation or rupture in a celebration. But while some people worry about the unified way in which a celebration unfolds, or about tranquility which allows recollection to happen, unusual kinds of music can also produce good effects—for example, distancing. They can open us up to what is beyond ourselves, to mystery, to the "unheard of," whereas a type of music that is too conventional can run the risk of wrapping us more tightly in our complacent habits.

However, we should not be systematically seeking types of "dislocatory" music, but rather we should be aware of the plus and minus values of surprise, and strive to achieve overall balance (see GL 5, p. 118, for St. Augustine's views on beauty and suitability).

30. Musical Instruments in the Liturgy (see p. 78)

A. Vatican II's Constitution on the Liturgy (no. 120)

1) acknowledges the privileged place that the pipe organ has acquired in Christian liturgy in the course of history;
2) accepts other musical instruments
   a) if they are capable of effectively fulfilling the liturgical role required of them,
   b) if they accord with the "dignity" of the place,
   c) if they really help the faithful to pray.

B. The Roman Instruction on Music in the Liturgy (8 March 1967) takes up the substance of the above, clarifying and adding to it (nos. 62-67):

1) the cultural context must be taken into account when deciding if a particular instrument is perceived as being compatible or not with Christian liturgy;
2) "all instruments admitted to worship will be used in such a way
   a) that they respond to the demands of the liturgical action,
   b) that they serve the beauty of the worship,
   c) and the edification of the faithful";
3) in certain cultures singing normally entails an instrumental accompaniment. This is allowable if the accompaniment
   a) supports the voices without drowning them, and
   b) "renders participation easier and the unity of the assembly deeper."

31. Musical Roles in the Assembly and Their Evolution
(see p. 52)

Two fundamental images have come down to us from the very beginnings of the church:

1. One of the members of the assembly proposes a chant to the assembly. So at Corinth, "when you are together, each one can have a *psalmos* [= a song]" said St. Paul (1 Cor 14:26).

2. The whole assembly is held together in the word and the Holy Spirit by all manner of chants, hymns, and spiritual songs (Eph 5:19).

By the fourth century three other images had emerged:

1. The image of the psalmist, a specialist reader whose role is to perform at the ambo the verses of the psalm, to which the assembly "responds" with a refrain.

2. The dialogue thus set up between the psalmist and all others.

3. The division of the assembly itself into two choirs which by turn pass the psalmic refrain from one to another (antiphony), and, later, do the same with *troparia*.

At the end of the seventh/beginning of the eighth centuries there appeared, from Mesopotamia to Spain, the "school" of cantors, from which would be born the liturgical *schola*. In the place of the dialogue between the psalmist (whose role had crumbled away) and the assembly (which had less and less to do in ritual singing) there was substituted dialogue between cantors, clerics or their equivalent, upon whom liturgical singing henceforward devolved. In the west, the evolution of sacred music would be linked to cantors, *scholae* and cathedral choirs, princes' courts, abbeys, chapters, and convents.

The liturgical cantillation of Latin texts having been formalized and fixed in musical "tones," the sacred ministers (celebrant, deacon, subdeacon) gained an important place in liturgical chant.

Thanks to the churches that issued from the Reformation, singing by assemblies was given back its value, using languages and forms of music familiar to the people. Even when sophisticated vocal and instrumental music developed in these churches, singing by the assembly still retained its primacy.

The printing of choir graduals and antiphonaries helped extend the role of cantors even into rural parishes of the Roman rite in the seventeenth and eighteenth centuries.

In the second half of the nineteenth century, parishes saw the development of chant "choirs," often polyphonic, as a reaction against operatic-style soloists who had infiltrated the churches. These were normally all-male choirs, but female choirs could also dialogue (from the nave) with choirs of cantors situated in the choir (properly speaking). Choir-lofts at the back of churches facilitated the creation of mixed choirs.

In the course of the twentieth century, the pastoral liturgical movement gradually regained its foothold in singing by assemblies. The Second Vatican Council gave its blessing to this movement. Singing by the gathered people was given primacy of place as being the most important means of participating in the sacred action. At the same time, the psalmist reappeared. Singing by the officiants was recalled as being something normal. The role of choirs was encouraged, without sexual discrimination. The door was wide open to the use of instruments, whether as an accompaniment or in a solo role.

32. New Humanity, A (see p. 107)

Paul said to the new Christians of Colossae: "You have stripped off the old humanity [RSV has "old self"], with its practices, and have clothed yourselves with the new humanity [RSV has "new self"], which is constantly being renewed, in order to come to knowledge, according to the image of its Creator" (Col 3:9-10). Let us try and clarify the meaning of this expression, one that is more mystic than moral. The *Traduction oecuménique de la Bible* (TOB) has the following note:

"The expression new humanity[6] is used to translate that radical transformation of being which is signified by baptism. The Old Testament announced the renewing of humankind under the influence of the Spirit which gives it a new heart capable of knowing God. By a new creation realized in Christ, who is the Second Adam and the image of the Father, humankind is led to its true humanity: it is created by God in justice and holiness and journeys through obedience toward true knowledge. This new humanity is a new humankind that goes beyond former distinc-

---

6. The whole of this passage, and indeed the title of this chapter itself, refers to *L'homme nouveau*—the new man—in the original French - translator's note.

tions of race, religion, culture and social class; it therefore has both a collective character (the church) and a personal character (the baptized person)" (TOB, pp. 607-8, note 9). Every eucharistic liturgy requires this birth in us of a new humanity, or our birth into this new body: "That we who share in the body and blood of Christ may be brought together in unity by the Holy Spirit" (Eucharistic Prayer II).

33. Operative Model (see p. 96)

Potters fashioning clay on the wheel have, both in their hands and in their spirits, different "models" from which to draw as many different varieties as they produce pots. The same is true for musicians and people who work in liturgy. As long as they are not simply producing a literal performance of a score or mechanically carrying out rubrics, they need, in order to produce living symbols, to be able ceaselessly to re-create music or festivity according to the "models" which underlie a particular piece or rite. Lying between the capability of doing so ("the art of . . .") and the practical execution ("this particular performance") there exists a model which is both the plan to be carried out and the "rules of the game" itself.

We can describe the operative model in liturgy as a symbolic channel that is familiar to the celebrating group, that has already been well absorbed by the group, and that is within the competence of those carrying it out. Such a model, often an unconscious one, allows the group to act in safety since the "game" and its rules are well known. But the model does not paralyze the action. Everything that happens appears to be spontaneous.

The use of the model involves either the whole group (which is capable of celebrating a festival, singing a hymn, acclaiming, processing, in a way which is full of meaning for the group) or individuals in the group (those capable of reading, singing psalmody, making announcements, presiding, providing accompaniment, etc.).

The idea and the use of the model can be applied either to a complete office (the Mass, the Paschal Vigil, etc.), or to ritual units (the liturgy of the word, opening rites, the eucharistic meal, etc.), or to elements within those units (a piece of psalmody, a litany, a presidential prayer, etc.).

Behaving creatively by following a model presupposes an apprenticeship. It is more than knowing what to do: it is *savoir-faire*.

34. Oral Traditions, Abandonment of (see p. 46)

Till recent times in western countries, when the printed word penetrated the whole of social life, the universal form of communication and cultural transmission in the human race was an oral one: from mouth to ear. This form often made use of rhythmic-melodic recitation techniques. In the Judaeo-Christian tradition the Bible—even though a book containing canonical writings (the Scriptures)—only reached believers by becoming a living word in biblical readings, preaching, forms of psalmody, and chants of all kinds.

The traditional position of the Roman liturgy experienced profound modification through the conjunction of two elements: (1) the use of Latin as a liturgical language which was no longer "spoken" but which people could read; (2) the status of the printed book as it became the unique canonical reference—the only material considered as "liturgical" was what the books approved by Rome contained. But such an evolution was only one aspect of a cultural change that affected the whole of the western world. Little by little in the course of the twentieth century, the transmission of knowledge abandoned all forms of oral culture and memorization--proverbs, tales and stories, question-answer forms, etc.—in favor of scientific experimentation and critical reflection. From now on, information regarding exclusively notional knowledge is stored in encyclopedias, specialized manuals, loose-leaf binders, and magnetic databanks.

But this evolution in conceptual knowledge leaves intact the additional human need to communicate with the senses, with "affectivity," according to human desires and fantasies. Love, art, and religion do not exist except "in the flesh." The poetic or biblical word does not exist without a "verbal body." Faith does not come without symbolic "stories" or "symbols" of faith. Prayer needs formulas that are known "by heart" and said with enjoyment.

A renewal of Christian worship—and evangelization—cannot take place without the re-finding and re-creation of oral forms of communication and expression, especially those that are included in the biblical tradition. The explosion of visual and aural mass media, far from replacing all these, serves simply to underline their loss. Poets and musicians are particularly involved in all this.

35. Organ in the Reformed Churches, The (see pp. 77 and 157)

Before the Reformation the organ had a solo role without being tied to singing by the assembly. What sort of a role could this wordless instrument play in a reformed style of worship? It varied greatly from reformer to reformer.

Luther welcomed the organ into worship so that this instrument might offer to God its own "personal" praise, inspired—like the praise of all the faithful—by the preaching of the Gospel (see (GL 4, p. 117) and by the themes of the liturgy and worship (never by worldly songs) when it was not actually treating a *cantus firmus*. Ecclesiastical regulations teach us that organists were paid because of the honor of music—indeed, they were sometimes better paid than the cantor (in the Lutheran sense) or director of music. In order to be a candidate for this position, the organist (who in villages was often also the sacristan, which does not in this case indicate that standards were rather low) had to have a solid musical formation and be capable of using the full resources of his (there were no female organists at this time) instrument, keeping it in good working order and ensuring its proper maintenance. There were no rules concerning the manner of playing: the organist's playing was expected to proclaim and give praise to the Lord.

Lutheran churches also welcomed lutes, viols, violas da gamba, recorders, krummhorns, trumpets, trombones and cornets. At the beginning of the seventeenth century, the *basso continuo* was taken by harpsichord, theorbo, and above all the lute. Wind instruments would be used to give color to a *cantus firmus* by supporting the choir, for example.

The organ in worship literally had a "respiratory" role in the sense that it played in alternation with the choir in the verses of the *Kyrie* and *Gloria*, as laid down in the Wittenberg regulations of 1536. The organ would follow the indications of the cantor. The choir had the musical pedagogical mission of teaching the chorale melody to the assembly; but as the melody was in the tenor part (cf. the first psalter of 1524 with its 5-part harmonizations) the assembly had some difficulty in following it. Gradually this choir role was replaced by the organ, and this is also how polyphony moved from voices to the organ. One work where we can see this evolution taking place appeared in 1650: Samuel Scheidt's (1557-1654) *100 Spiritual Songs Harmonized for the Organ*. This new role for the organ had also been in evidence in Scheidt's *Tabulatura Nova* of 1624, whose third section is a complete set of organ pieces for the whole liturgical year. It is worth noting that both Scheidt and Frescobaldi also wrote profane organ works as well.

A single generation separates Scheidt from Bach (1685-1750). According to Albert Schweitzer, the spread of organ music in the Reformed Churches was due to the chorale, which contained the seeds of unlimited development. Preluding on and accompanying the chorale stimulated organists to solve technical difficulties. The chorale melodies had a solid shape and a well-defined rhythm which asked for contrapuntal treatment. This work was accomplished in the space of three generations of organist-composers: Scheidt, Pachelbel, Buxtehude, and J.S. Bach. Scheidt was the first to notate his pieces in the Italian manner. He brought out the chorale melody in all voice parts—bass, tenor, alto, and soprano—and was the first to exploit the contrast of different stops. Pachelbel, Böhm, Reinken, and Buxtehude (c.1637-1707) among others created different chorale forms for the organ. Bach heard and knew all these men except Pachelbel. Buxtehude made use of all types of chorale for organ, but his favorite form was the chorale fantasia. It was left to Bach to discover that the chorale prelude remains imperfect to the extent that the words do not come to life, for in hearing a melody in a prelude the text is ineluctably present in the spirit and the depths of faith of the listeners. The chorales in the *Orgelbüchlein* are fantasias on a descriptive motif that contains the main theme inspiring the text. But the Leipzig Cantor only used this procedure when the text naturally lent itself to it. This deeply spiritual harmony between the melodies and the words of the organ chorales has left its mark on generations of the faithful right up to the present day. The organ truly gives forth its personal praise in worship rendered to the Lord in his church.

In Holland the organ was banned from worship, and this resulted in organ concerts being given outside the times of worship. We do not know if Sweelinck was Reformed, or Lutheran, or

Catholic. It was the burghers who asked the preachers for the organ to introduce the psalm chants as early as 1632. Calvin saw nothing more in the organ than a vain instrument. For him, instruments were good at the time of the Law in the Temple, but now that believers had attained adulthood in Christ they no longer needed instruments. It was not till 1731 that the organ returned to Berne; in Zurich it was even later: 1839 in the Neumünster, 1855 in the Fraumünster, and 1876 in the Grossmünster.

Luther did not reject the liturgical use of bells, but he restricted them to calling the faithful together for worship, for matins and vespers, to signal the approach of enemies, and as a fire warning. He acknowledged their use for prayers for peace. At burials, small or large bells were used according to the social standing of the dead person. Right up to the present, bells are rung on Saturday evening as a preparation for Sunday worship. In our own time, liturgies of consecration of bells still bear witness to the role of bells in liturgical and social life.

36. Organum (see p. 46)

In antiquity and the early Middle Ages this term designated various instruments as well as the human voice. Later on, organum marked the first steps taken in polyphony: it grew out of the superimposition on the *vox principalis* [the "tenor"] of a new voice-part (*vox organalis*) at the interval of a fourth or a fifth. At first running parallel, the voices subsequently intertwined in the form known as *discantus* (duplum, triplum, quadruplum) in the ninth century. In the twelfth century, different "schools" were using melismatic organum: the most famous included St. Martial at Limoges and Notre-Dame in Paris, both of which created vocal ornamentation on the principal chant. This soon led to the integration of French words (whence we get the term motet, from the French *mot*, meaning "word"). Later on, barred rhythm supplanted modal rhythm (towards 1250—see *Ars antiqua*).

37. Orthodox Church, Liturgical Music in the (see p. 77)

"The sacerdotal college and the faithful form a single liturgical body in which each person has his or her proper function. This human unity explains why the Orthodox have never admitted the use, in church, of musical instruments, of sounds without words, precisely because the church considers that the human voice alone can be clothed with the dignity of responding to the word of God and that the "choir" which sings with a single voice is the most adequate expression of the Body, united to the angelic choir."

Paul Evdokimov, L'Orthodoxie,
Delachaux & Niestlé, 1959, p. 240

"The ecclesial community is a hierarchical community. But this in no way signifies that some are greater than others: it means that each person has his or her place and role in respect of the gifts each has received and in respect to the needs of the community. And everyone has need of everyone else: no person is excluded or exists of him-/herself.

"A further implication deriving from the two preceding statements is the necessity for the person with the ministry of singing, whether composer or cantor, to be truly at the service of the community. This means that these ministers must not interpose themselves between the word and the community, not only by the unintelligible character of the composition or its performance but by the fact of imposing on others the ministers' own individual psychological sensitivities, however interesting the latter may be. All this implies a school of learning, a very stringent and difficult discipline.

"If it is clear that by virtue of the link between word and music a liturgical composer must avoid composing in a way that draws all attention toward the music and the harmony by turning attention away from the word, it is much more difficult for the composer (as for every artist) to strip away from him- or herself a sort of self-awareness in his or her art, replacing this self-awareness by an awareness of the church, in order that it become what one theologian has called a Catholic awareness—in other words to efface oneself in order that one's composition might approach more closely to the fullness of the word, to the "silence" which is in the word.

"There are musical forms which do not fit well with liturgical expression. So, purely instrumental music is not admitted in the Eastern and Western Orthodox traditions. Contrary to what some people think, this kind of music does not help promote unity of spirit by creating a certain harmonious atmosphere outside the word. Quite the reverse: appealing to aesthetic emotion detached from unanimous prayer runs the risk of dispersing such a harmonious atmosphere."

Nicolas Lossky, "Quelques
réflexions sur la musique liturgique" in
the journal *Contacts*, no. 113, pp. 58-59.

38. Poetic Language (see p. 66)

The poet Patrice de la Tour du Pin once said: "Poetry can be recognized by the fact that it never reaches the end of the [printed] line." This was not just a simple witticism on his part, nor is it a refusal to define the indefinable: poetry. What he was doing was jokingly recognizing that poetry is something which creates a space around the words in order to give these words the opportunity to say something more than themselves, to allow them to interplay and indeed play off one against another. Poetic language is play. In the same way that music is not just notes but what is "between" the notes, so poetry is to be found in the gaps between the words.

If the liturgy is the *locus* of mystery, the place where mystery is proclaimed, contemplated, celebrated, and sung—the mystery of God, humanity, and the world—it is evident that the liturgy needs poetic language in order to be what it needs to be. Scripture teaches us that our liturgy is grafted onto The Book in which, in the Old Testament, God speaks through the medium of God's poets, from Job to Malachi; or, in his Gospel, the poet Jesus of Nazareth announces in parables the wonders of the Father and of the Kingdom; or, in the Book of Revelation, the poet John makes us contemplate the invisible. Poetry—in the creation narratives of Genesis, in the genealogies of the Gospel, in the Our Father and the Beatitudes, in the canticle of the Virgin Mary.

In order to echo this word of the Poet-God, it is normal that in the prayers and chants of the liturgy a word from the Poet-Man is raised up. In this way a people can respond to its God with words that speak of its faith—in other words, which speak of what they know: with words that speak of hope, which is "more than they need"; with words that speak of charity, which is "more than they thought it possible to love." Perhaps in this way we can escape the severe judgment of Jesus, the poet who invites us to play:

> We played the flute,
> but you wouldn't dance.
> We sang funeral dirges,
> but you wouldn't beat your breasts.
>
> (Mt 11:16)

39. Presidency (see p. 50)

All liturgically-constituted assemblies have at their head a presider. In English-speaking countries this term is generally preferred to that of president, the latter having a particular political or administrative meaning in our society. Because even presider can seem offensive to some, many prefer to use the term celebrant, but we should note that this term is not sufficiently precise; every Christian member of an assembly is a celebrant; in a very real sense we are all concelebrants in liturgy, whether ordained or not. Whatever the case, the noun presidency has not so far been ousted by neologisms such as "presider-ship."

We can find this term cited several times as early as the New Testament. For example, 1 Timothy 5:17 speaks of the "elders who know well how to exercise presidency"; and in the second century, the Second Apology of Justin describes the role of the *proestos* during eucharist. So we are talking about a function for which there is already good evidence in primitive liturgies.

The Greek *proistanai* is rendered in Latin by *praeesse*—literally, to be ahead of, to be at the head of. In the church it is Christ who is the Head of Christians. In the liturgy this "capital" truth is manifested through the presidential function.

From patristic writings of the fourth and fifth centuries, as well as the earliest sacramentaries, we can sum up the presidential function as follows:

• open and conclude the celebration, which means that the presider leads the celebration and thus guarantees its authenticity. The presider establishes the link between the different parts of the celebration, between the different ministers or "actors," and the link with the assembly;

• proclaim the word of God, especially in the homily;

• take on the prayers which are part of this role and pronounce them in the name of everyone (as distinct from the prayers that the presiders says together with all his brothers and sisters).

During the Middle Ages the liturgy became adapted to the customs of the imperial courts; and so the role of the presider assumed a more solemn style. At the same time, little by little, the presider found himself isolated in the middle of pontifical chapels, cut off from the assembly. Incomprehensible liturgical language, the altar further and further away, mystic gestures—all these obscured the presidential function. Liturgical prayer, with the presider's back turned to the assembly, thus became the sole province of clerics sent crazy with ever-increasing swarms of abstruse rubrics (especially from the Council of Trent onward). Deprived, as it were, of an authentic presidential word, the assembly became the place for pious ancillary practices.

Certainly there was the Tridentine reform; and we should emphasize that it restored scriptural preaching. But because the reform's principal work was to combat the reformers, it steered clear of any gesture which could be interpreted by the reformers as a concession—such as liturgy in the language of the people, which was desired by many of the Council Fathers at Trent. The church had to wait until Vatican II for the presider, in the Roman liturgy, to rediscover the assembly and make a communal prayer out of the prayer of all.

40. Psalmist, The (see p. 56)

At the time when responsorial psalmody developed (fourth century), a more specialized role of reader-reciter-cantor separated itself from the function of the reader. This new minister was capable of cantillating the verses of the psalms from the ambo in such a way that the assembly could interpolate its refrain.

This practice had a great effect on the psalms. From now on psalms were interposed between the readings at Mass, alternated with readings during vigils, and began the people's morning and evening offices. Like the reader, the psalmist was "instituted" or "ordained" by the bishop and was part of the local clergy.

The function of the psalmist quickly fell into disuse. This occurred at the same time as the people's participation in the singing collapsed and the responsorial psalm form atrophied (leaving only a single verse behind). More specialized cantors and scholas succeeded the psalmist.

By restoring the responsorial psalm to the Mass, the reform of Vatican II also *ipso facto* restored the function of the psalmist (General Instruction on the Roman Missal, nos. 36 and 90; see no. 67 where competence is demanded and no. 316 which gives a reminder about preparation before the office).[7] By analogy the function of the psalmist is to be extended to other instances of psalmody where this role can be useful.

41. "Pure" Music (see p. 85)

The concept of music that grew out of nineteenth-century romanticism left behind it an idea planted in the mentality of the bourgeois. This mentality revolved around seemliness and decency, and the idea that a form of "pure" music existed.

We can easily see that this idea actually means a kind of music . . . which is nothing but music. In other words, a kind of music whose sole task is to make music and to produce in society the obvious pleasure that comes from the simple fact of listening to "good" music.

But what kind of music could qualify as "pure" under these criteria? Moreover, what would one call a type of music that is not "pure"? Should it be called "impure"?

According to the criteria outlined above, Beethoven's D major Violin Concerto would be "pure" music but, equally obviously, not a single measure of Monteverdi (who wrote for the Prince of Mantua, and later for St. Mark's in Venice), nor a single measure of Bach (who wrote for the Prince of Anhalt-Köthen, King Frederick the Great of Prussia, and, of course, for the faithful in St. Thomas' Church, Leipzig) would qualify.

So what is pure music?

What we are actually dealing with here is a concept which has no aesthetic power whatsoever. Music is always used for something.

Music, whether it be a Breton folk dance, a rock number, or an extract from the *Rite of Spring*, can make people dance. Music, whether it be a Bach cantata, an organ piece by Lefebure-Wély, or

---

7. It was the revival of the responsorial psalm and the psalmist which led very rapidly to the revival of the ministry of the cantor in England at the beginning of the 1970s, but this process had in fact already begun with the publication in 1969 of an English translation of the *Graduale Simplex* (edited by John Ainslie, published by Geoffrey Chapman). The General Instruction of the Roman Missal no. 78, which states that the norm for every Mass is that the presider be accompanied by a lector, a cantor and at least one server (in that order of priority), was also influential.

a *Dominus vobiscum*, can accompany a rite. Music, whether it be an opera by Verdi or one by Wagner, can fit with a theatrical scene.

But what is it doing when it has no other end in view than simply to be music for music's sake? Or to put it another way, what is the purpose of a Beethoven string quartet?

Commenting on Alembert's *Discours préliminaire de l'encyclopédie*, the philosopher-musicologist Catherine Kintzler says the following in her book on Jean-Philippe Rameau (to celebrate the three-hundreth anniversary of his birth):

The application of the criterion of finality allows the foundation of the division into sciences and arts, science being the application of reason to an object in order to produce knowledge, whereas art is the application of reason to an object in order to produce usefulness and practicality.

> Jean-Philippe Rameau: *Splendeur et naufrage de l'esthétique du plaisir à l'âge classique*[8]

In other words, have those who speak about "pure" music reflected sufficiently on what they are talking about? (See also Jean Molino, "Fondement symbolique de l'expérience esthétique" in *Analyse musicale*, 3rd semester, 1986/11.)

42. Reader, The (see p. 56)

The function of the reader[9] began at the same time as Christian assemblies themselves, since the reading of Scripture (at first the Law and the Prophets, then the writings of the apostles and evangelists) is a constituent part of Christian worship.

Referring to the cultural context, we could add:

1) that the function of the public reader gave rise to an apprenticeship;
2) that this function normally devolved on anyone who knew how to fulfill it;
3) that for "public speaking" there were "tones" and "rhythms" (but not in our current "musical" sense);
4) that in the case of sacred Scripture, reading could not be carried out in a banal and familiar fashion. "Whoever reads the Bible without cantillating it," says the Mishnah, "is an idolator."

---

8. Pub. Le Sycomore, 1983, p. 202
9. The term "reader" is used in more countries than the term "lector."

The ministry of reader appeared clearly in the third century. The reader was "instituted" or "ordained" in the community when the bishop handed the book to him. The ministry became one of the "clerical orders." The task was often entrusted to young boys who had clear voices and who could be formed in *ad hoc* schools.

Whereas the function and the order of reader lasted in the churches of the east, in the west the reader's function fell into disuse when the Scriptures were no longer explained to the people (sixth century) and the order of lector became a stage on the way to priesthood. From this time on, the readings at Mass were done by the higher orders. Tones for recitation were stylized and became a musical recitative.

By once again giving value to the role of the Bible in celebration, the liturgical renewal restored the function of the reader. In 1972 the ministry of "lector" was officially re-established in the Roman rite: the reader is now publicly instituted in the community by means of the sign of the handing-over of the book.[10]

43. Repertoires of the Reformed Churches (see p. 43)

For Calvin (1509-1564) there could be no praise of God without an awareness of the content of praise. For Luther (1483-1546) on the other hand, all of nature sang the glory of God, and the very flowers and birds had the Gospel inscribed in their throats. Calvin recognized that singing possessed "the great force and vigor of moving and inflaming the hearts of men" to invoke and praise God. He advocated simple music so that it could be understood and sung by both children and adults in the temple, in the fields, and in the home. Calvin, rejecting polyphony as being made for entertaining the ears, preferred unison singing, and only allowed

---

10. In some English-speaking countries this has yet to happen. England has not yet adopted the Rite of Institution of Readers, and the Canadian Bishops' Conference have refused to do so until the order of readers is open to women as well as men. In the United States the Institution of Readers has been adopted by only one diocese; elsewhere in the country it is limited to students preparing for presbyteral ordination, due to the restriction to male readers. In the *Book of Blessings* the Order for the Blessing of Readers (Chapter 61) and the Order for the Blessing of Musicians (Chapter 62) provide a nonexclusive service which is more widely used.

the psalms as texts. He personally translated six palms and the Canticle of Simeon so that they could be set to music. Clément Marot (1496-1544) translated forty-nine psalms, plus the Canticle of Simeon. The success of the collection in which these appeared was such that Francis I, in 1533, agreed to be its patron. Its language was indeed admirable. Marot was also the author of *Saints Cantiques* (1595) which used scriptural texts set to anonymous melodies.

Theodore de Bèze (1519-1605) was a less gifted writer who paraphrased the remainder of the psalms. Loys Bourgeois (1510-1557) was both a musical theoretician and a cantor (at the Cathedral of St. Peter in Geneva). In his *Droict Chemin de musique* ("Correct Musical Pathway") he set out the principles of sol-fa, of notation, and of singing the psalms. Approximately eighty-eight melodies were composed by him. (Today churches everywhere still regularly sing his melody known as the Old 100th.) Claude Goudimel (1520-1572) set four versions of the psalter to music and also composed five four-part Masses, three Magnificats, and ten motets.

The registers of the company of pastors at Geneva in 1542 attests to psalm-singing by children and adults alike. Even today, reformed worship still includes psalm-singing of these very same melodies, with a modernized version of the texts; and these melodies have also inspired certain Catholic authors.

The history of the psalter was played out at Geneva, Strasbourg, and Lyon in turn. In the end it was the Geneva tradition that prevailed.

1539 Strasbourg: *Auculns Pseaulmes et cantiques mys en chant* ("Some Psalms and Canticles Set for Singing"), thirteen psalms versified by Marot.

1542 Geneva: *La Forme des prières et chants ecclésiastiques* ("The Form of the Ecclestical Prayers and Chants"), thirty psalms versified by Marot on new melodies.

1546 Paris: *Premier Livre contenant 31 Pseaulmes: Livre second contenant 17 Pseaulmes* ("First Book Containing 31 Psalms; Second Book containing 17 Psalms") (set to music in four parts).

1547 Lyon: *Pseaulmes cinquante de David, 4 parties à voix de contrepoint égal consonant au verbe* ("Fifty Psalms of David, 4-Voice Equal Counterpoint Consonant with the Text"—i.e., note against note) . . .

1562 Geneva: *Pseaumes de David (150)* ("Psalms of David (150)":
official collection, complete corpus paraphrased and provided
with melodies, 30,000 copies published (rhyming texts by Marot
and de Bèze).

1565 Lausanne: Guillaume Franc's *Le Psautier complet avec le
chant de l'Église de Lausanne* ("The Complete Psalter with the
Chants of the Church of Lausanne").

1583 Geneva: *Les Psaumes de David (à 4, 5, 6, 7, 8 parties)* ("The
Psalms of David (in 4, 5, 6, 7, 8 parts)), Paschal de l'Estocart.
Concert style.

In *La musique protestante de langue française* Edith Weber cites
twenty-seven editions of the psalter in the years 1539 to 1627.
Notable was the absence of bar-lines which made for flexible
utterance. Binary and ternary rhythms alternated, and syncopations were used. The 1976 Lausanne collection *Psaumes et Cantiques*,
remaining faithful to this tradition, still does not use bar-lines in
the psalms.

Luther possessed musical *ars et scientia*—scholars agree on
this—coupled with an extraordinary creative power. As Luther
himself said, he had the gift of listening to the language of the
people, of "looking people straight in the mouth," and of reproducing this language in a clear and natural manner. Being a
humanist pedagogue, he was able to realize the threefold entity of
School-Church-Music by entrusting to the cantor the task of
teaching the psalms, the chorales, and the responses, as well as
instrumental music, to children in school. More advanced pupils
formed a *Knabenchor* or a *Mädchenchor* (boys' and girls' choirs), and
these choirs embellished worship on feastdays by performing
motets, sometimes accompanied by wind instruments. In Germany, popular song was sung by everyone. Luther did not hold
popular or profane music in disdain, but said "Why should the
Devil have all the best tunes?" and freely adapted from this
repertoire. He also selected, adapted, and translated medieval
Latin hymns. He collaborated closely with the musician-liturgist
Johann Walter (or Walther) (1496-1570), and submitted all his
output to Walter's scrutiny during the time that he was working
toward a Mass in which the assembly could participate through
prayers and singing. Thanks to Walter, three small collections
appeared in 1524: *Achtliederbuch* ("Book with Eight Songs"), eight
texts for four melodies; *Enchiridion oder Handbüchlein* ("Manual or

Handbook") with twenty-five texts and fifteen melodies; and *Geistliches Gesangbüchlein* ("Spiritual Songbook") with thirty-eight polyphonic pieces and five *cantiones* in Latin, three for 6 voices, on chorale melodies, using *cantus firmus* technique, designed for use by choirs. Luther is credited with some thirty-seven chorales (the best-known in the English-speaking world are probably *Vom Himmel hoch* and *Ein' feste Burg*—the "Reformation Chorale"). He wrote to Spalatin, "We are looking everywhere for poets."

Luther also called upon the services of C. Rupsch (c.1475-c.1530). Toward 1530 Ludwig Senfl (1490-1543) composed Masses and motets in something approaching the Franco-Flemish style. He was a Catholic, but Luther preferred his work to that of all others. Senfl created chorale melodies, placing the melody in the tenor; his counterpoint was rich and varied; he also drew inspiration from Latin hymns and popular songs.

Martin Agricola (1486-1556) produced excellent theoretical works, the best being the *Musica instrumentalis deutsch* (1529) ("German Treatise on Instrumental Music"). In 1541 he published *Ein Sangbüchlein aller Sonntag Evangelia* ("A Songbook of All the Sunday Gospels").

It would be the task of the second generation of musicians (1550-1600) and then the third generation (seventeenth century) to forge a form of liturgical music suited to the worshiping assembly. Some made use of the new style of simple counterpoint, and gradually the *cantus firmus* passed from the tenor to the soprano part. It was Lucas Osiander (1534-1604) who promoted the widespread use of the new style in church singing. For the schools and churches of Würtemburg he published in 1586 *Cinquante chorals et psaumes à quatre voix* ("Fifty Chorales and Psalms for Four Voices"), in counterpoint, set to music in such a way that the whole of a Christian assembly is able (absolutely!) to participate in the singing. He placed the melody in the soprano part.

In 1574 Johannes Eccard (1553-1611) wrote his *40 deudsche Christliche Liedlein* ("40 German Christian Little Songs") (for 4 voices) and *20 neue Christliche Gesänge* ("20 New Christian Songs") (also for 4 voices). He placed the melody in the soprano and accompanied it with rich harmonies. The work of Melchior Vulpius (c.1570-1615) was distinguished by an extremely simple style. His chorales are still in present-day repertoires [in the English-speaking world, for example, the hymn-tune Vulpius (*Gelobt sei Gott*)]. As for Michael Praetorius (c.1571-1621), he was familiar with the directions being taken in Italian musical style. Between 1605 and 1610 he published his nine-volume *Musae Sionae*. It contained 1248 chorales with 537 melodies, set *"notam contra notam"* in simple counterpoint. (His best-known setting is probably the Christmas hymn *Es ist ein' Ros' entsprungen*.) Hans Leo Hassler was a musician of immense ability who opened the way for German musicians to complete their musical formation in Italy. He himself studied with Andrea Gabrieli in Venice, and his is the standard harmonization used for Luther's chorale *Ein' feste Burg*. (He was also the composer of the melody to "O Sacred Head" known as the Passion Chorale.) In 1607 he published *Psalmen und christliche Gesänge mit 4 Stimmen auf die Melodien Fugweis komponiert* ("Psalms and Christian Songs for 4 Voices Composed in Fugato Style"), and in 1608 and 1637 *Kirchengesänge, Psalmen und geistliche Lieder auf die gemeinen Melodien mit 4 Stimmen Simpliciter gesetzt* ("Church Songs, Psalms, and Spiritual Songs on Familiar Melodies Set in Simple Fashion for 4 Voices"). From his pen also flowed Masses and motets for performance in the private chapel of the Emperor Rudolf.

To the third generation belongs Crüger (1598-1662). His chorale melodies are still sung in our churches today [e.g., *Nun danket alle Gott*—Now Thank We All Our God], and we owe to him the existence of many published collections of chorales, especially his *Praxis Pietatis Melica* which went through forty editions. By the third edition the contents amounted to 387 chorales with 170 melodies. Crüger also wrote settings of *Laudes vespertinae*, Magnificat settings, and some important treatises. Heinrich Schütz (1585-1672) is generally considered to be the "Father of German Protestant music." In Venice he discovered the madrigal and instrumental music, and subsequently returned to Italy where he was in contact with the Monteverdi circle. His many compositions are still in widespread use today. (Details on another composer from this generation, Samuel Scheidt, will be found in GL 35, p. 144.)

The Pietist period (1675-1750) sacrificed the proclamation of the Gospel in favor of individual piety. Chants were addressed to the soul of the believer, expressed repentance, and invited the believer to an examination of conscience. (For J.S. Bach, see GL 35, p. 144.)

The period of Reawakening (1800-1900) produced spiritual songs that were less solid, rather lighter in content. The texts were generally of greater worth than the melodies; and the chorale evolved no further but instead became the prey of romanticism and subjectivism. The Swiss reformers placed stress on the vernacular language, even dialect language (a dialect collection was published in Zurich in 1536 and 1540 and distributed by Johannes Zwick (c.1496-1542): *Nüw gsangbüchli von vil schönen Psalmen und geistlichen liedern* ("New Little Songbook with Many Beautiful Psalms and Spiritual Songs"). Their aim was above all the proclamation of objective faith (through the *Bekenntnislied* [the "Credal Song"]), though Ambrosius Laurer left much more room for fantasy in this respect.

44. Reprise (see p. 95)

This is a technical device on the printed page in a responsory, which shows the singers precisely to what point in a text the singers have to go back. At the end of a verse the reprise is most often indicated by printing the first two or three words of the responsorialized fragment. (To achieve the same effect, certain plainchant manuscripts used the letter P, an abbreviation for *presa*, i.e., "reprise.")

The following is an example of a reprise—the short responsory at compline:

R/   *In manus tuas, Domine,* * *commendo spiritum meum.* In
manus.
V/   *Redemisti nos, Domine, Deus veritatis.*
* Commendo spiritum meum.
Gloria Patri. In manus.

In fact the reprise is a sort of refrain, but in the context of a chant which is more in the order of a recitative than a song-form.

45. Rite and Form (see p. 88)

The form is the "given" which allows one to see, to hear, to taste, etc. The form, as an aspect of the rite that involves the senses, is situated between ritual function ("Here, we are singing in order to . . .") and signification, defined as a reality symbolically aimed at through faith (adoration, meditation, thanksgiving, etc.).

In the chain "function-form-signification," everything is transmitted by means of a form perceivable by the senses, by an "aesthetic" sense of what constitutes the rite as a symbolic act.

The form can be perceived at several levels.

1. At the operative level: "This type of music is good for . . ." or "not so good for . . ." (walking in procession, proclaiming a message, savoring a text, bringing about a dialogue or an acclamation, creating an atmosphere). At this operative level, the suitability of the form can be analyzed from a technical point of view: direct form, responsorial form, form with refrain, strophic form; one-unit form, binary form, ternary form; vocal tessitura, melodic contours, rhythmic figurations. Each element can be checked off with regard to the function that is to be fulfilled.

2. At the global level of suitability or non-suitability ("This music helps people to pray . . ."—"We can't pray with this kind of music"), of ethos (sensual or spiritual), of aesthetics (beautiful or ugly), of acknowledged value (good quality or worthless), of norms (allowed or forbidden), and so on.

At the first level it is above all specialists who contribute: composers, those responsible for liturgies, choir directors, animators, performers. At the second level it should be above all the faithful and pastors who contribute.

46. Sacred Music—Liturgical Music (see pp. 38, 86, 103, and 118)

Of what music can it be said: "This is sacred music"? The answer appears to be simple: the Mass in B minor, Gregorian chant, Mozart's Requiem . . . All this is sacred music. Things get a little more complicated when we ask if there is a difference between sacred music and profane music; and things become completely insoluble if we try to find the musical characteristics distinguishing one from the other. The problem really becomes clear once we learn that the orchestral music used by Monteverdi to embellish the "*Deus in adjutorium*" of his Vespers of the Blessed Virgin is none other than a borrowing from the prologue to his opera *Orfeo,* or that the famous aria "*Bereite dich, Zion*" from Bach's Christmas Oratorio comes from a profane cantata, *Die Wahl des Hercules,* composed the previous year.

Perhaps we might think that we are on safer ground with Gregorian chant. Yes, if you hear the chant performed by the monks of Solesmes; not at all, if it is performed by one of the early music groups that presents restorations according to the latest musicological discoveries in the area of Gregorian chant. Does, then, sacred music really exist?

Catholics who have taken over the term "sacred music" for their own ends would be astonished to learn that the term first appeared in the Lutheran-Protestant world of North Germany—more precisely in the title of a work of Michael Praetorius dating from 1614. Here it is not a question of categorizing works, nor one of defining the properties of certain pieces: the first part of Praetorius' encyclopedia is consecrated to *"musica sacra et ecclesiastica."*[11]

It was at the end of the eighteenth and the beginning of the nineteenth centuries that the notion of sacred music began to be used in the Catholic Church—thus it is a recent idea. A movement was born which aimed at combatting the progressive theatricalization of music used at High Mass, especially in South Germany and its neighbor Austria. This movement preached a return to *die heilige Musik* ("holy music"), to *musica sacra*. The term first appeared in an official church document at the provincial Synod of Cologne, and the movement reached its fulfillment in 1868 when Fr. Franz Witt founded the *Allgemeiner Cäcilienverband* (the "Universal Caecilian Association"). As early as 1870, "Caecilianism" received approval from the Holy See at the hands of Pius IX himself, in the following terms:

• sacred music must be distinguished from profane music;
• sacred music is that which is "appropriate for the majesty of the rites";
• the authentic and indispensable *musica sacra* is constituted by ancient music (the *stile antico* and the *prima prattica*), and especially by Gregorian chant and the polyphony of Palestrina.

It was within these two repertoires that musicians would henceforth have to search for music to be sung in the offices of the church, and it was from these that musicians would draw their inspiration if they wanted to compose works of beauty. Thus Liszt's work was rejected on account of its chromaticism, but Don Lorenzo Perosi would still be writing well into the twentieth century in the style of . . . Palestrina.

---

11. This section is indebted to the work of Nicolas Schalz, Professor of Musicology at the University of Bremen and a member of *Universa Laus*. For further details, see *La Maison-Dieu*, 108, 131, 164.

It was this notion of sacred music, along with its desire to purify church music but also carrying in its train a complete conservationist ideology, which would receive ratification from

- Pius X's motu proprio *Tra le sollecitudini* of 1903: "A musical composition for the church is that much more sacred and liturgical the closer it approaches Gregorian melody in its movement, its inspiration and its feeling" (II:3);

  - Pius XII's encyclical *Musicae Sacrae Disciplina* of 1955;
  - the instruction *De Musica Sacra* of 1958.

There are some subtle distinctions, however. Pius XII's encyclical, and above all the 1958 instruction, would considerably broaden the notion of sacred music: "By sacred music is to be understood Gregorian chant, sacred polyphony, modern sacred music, sacred music for organ, popular religious chants and religious music" (*De Musica Sacra*, no. 4).

Vatican II's Constitution on the Sacred Liturgy keeps the term "sacred music" but gives it a very different meaning and content: "Sacred music will be the more holy the more closely it is linked with the liturgical action" (SC 112). What defines the holiness of sacred music is none other than its capability to allow the realization of the demands of the liturgical action in which it plays a part. So, while keeping the term, the council saved it from ideology by reinserting in it the notion of *aptum* (appropriateness, coherence, connection, as the constitution puts it) that the ancients from the time of St. Augustine (see GL 5, p. 118) held as the principal qualifying criterion of music in the liturgy.

Having said this, the notion of "sacred music" still remains an imprecise one, as its history shows.

- It is a nebulous notion: so many different kinds of music can be classified under this heading that it has no real pertinence, whether religious or musical. Furthermore, the content is completely different, depending on whether one is in the domain of ethnomusicology or a Roman document. The church has the right to have its own definition, but this definition must be consistent with musical science, and this is not the case.
- It is a notion with geographical and historical limitations. Here we are talking about a "certain idea" of church music produced by a particular group in a given historical period and in a precise geographical region.

• It is an ambiguous notion. The sacred belongs to the whole of humanity; it is not Christian in itself; it can even be pagan. And we know how rigorously the New Testament eliminated (when talking about liturgy) all cultic vocabulary in order that the specifically Christian liturgical action should not be confused with actions in Jewish or pagan worship.

This is why, within the logic of the definition of Vatican II, the *Universa Laus* document prefers to speak of "Christian liturgical music" or "Christian ritual music."[12]

47. Singing (see p. 73)

The act of singing is a single action, global and unified, even if we know that it results from the complex interplay of numerous elements deriving from the body, from the intelligence, from sensitivity and from the entire personality of the singer.

In the same way, a sung composition is a unique object made up of text and music that are inseparable, in such a way that the quality of a chant is measured—among other criteria—by the power of the links which unite the text and the music. This quality can be discerned at a number of different levels:

(a) The global appeal of the chant, the overall impression that it gives us: e.g., the deep coherence between a Protestant chorale and a solid text that affirms faith, or the unity of a psalm of praise with the lively joy of music that dances. In the most successful chants, the principal quality derives from a strong formal and fundamental correspondence between text and music.

(b) The melody, and the way in which it gives value and heightens the meaning of the text, the intention and movement of the text, the sonority of the syllables, the rhymes: this is achieved by means of melodic intervals (ascending or descending) and their span, and by whether they recur regularly or at random.

(c) The rhythm, and the way in which the syllables of the words are separated or linked together, lengthened or shortened in order to correspond with the accents of the particular language, and in order to make the text "speak."

---

12. For an extensive treatment of the clarification of terms in English, see Edward Foley's "Music, Liturgical" in *The New Dictionary of Sacramental Worship*, ed. by Peter E. Fink (Collegeville: The Liturgical Press, 1990) 854-870.

48. Singing, Act of (see p. 86)

The desire to express ourselves through music is deeply rooted in our culture, despite certain completely theoretical declarations by some musicians and philosophers.

First, in every act of listening to music there is normally an affective and phantasmique (the physical aspect) projection, and at the same time a representation of human passions or of other cognitive constituents (the symbolic aspect). Active singing, moreover, takes on both a somatic [bodily] dimension (voice, motor function, etc.) and an identity (the "I" of the chant is the "I" of the one who is singing). This is the source of the old adage *Qui bene cantat, bis orat* ("Those who sing well pray twice"). But there is also ambiguity here: the person who sings "speaks twice" and/or "speaks and also does not speak," since he or she "displays the act of speaking."

We need to make a clear distinction between the text that we sing and the act of singing.

In singing, a verbal text is absorbed in a poetic "doing" which does not primarily mean ordinary verbal communication. Old sayings such as "It's only a song" express this loss of significant weight in the sung word. It is quite normal to sing a love song or a battle song without in any way being involved, or feeling oneself involved, in this "love" or "war."

In an act of singing, we can simulate, parody, or even contradict the meaning of the text we are singing.

At any rate, getting assemblies to sing is a demanding thing and an ambiguous thing, if it is a question of identifying oneself so deeply, body and soul, in the song: we should be aware of this.

49. Singing, Charism of (see p. 56)

A person who possesses the qualities of being a solo singer places his or her gifts at the service of the prayer and the song of the celebrating assembly. For this reason the role and the attitude of the solo singer in the liturgy cannot be reduced to those adopted in the concert hall or on public occasions. But this "spirituality," so important for the celebration, does not replace the necessary technical and vocal qualities of the soloist: it presupposes them. Moreover, the solo singer who is truly and completely at the service of music and text of quality—without wanting to "possess" the listeners, nor tempted to turn the communal action to his or her own advantage—is close to entering the musical area that is proper to Christian celebration.

50. Singing by the Assembly, Failure to Appreciate (see pp. 54 and 60)

The fundamental reason for singing by the assembly is still often misunderstood, and from a number of points of view:

• by certain composers, who see in the assembly's singing an impoverishment of the repertoire used in the liturgy, their only point of reference being certain sophisticated forms of musical writing;

• by choirs of a preconciliar type, who feel that their monopoly is threatened by this novelty;

• by assemblies themselves, who have often not understood the reason for this form of participation. Often Christians simply believe that "chants" are needed in a celebration: they tolerate taking on this role themselves in the context of an assembly without a choir, but believe that they should cease as soon as a group is present which is able to carry out this musical function better than they can.

This failure to appreciate the value of singing by the assembly should not astonish us. First, community singing is scarcely a part of contemporary social practice (apart from the rare exceptions of pop singers who are now beginning to involve their audiences). Second, outside the liturgy, composers are almost never asked to write with this aim in mind. In the church itself, the abandonment of singing by the assembly for many centuries has provoked a rupture the repairing of which will doubtless take a long time. Third, parishes attempted congregational singing without the pastor, musician, or parish prepared liturgically. The result was a number of poor experiences, extending over several years. These ugly half-hearted efforts resulted in a bad experience for a number of people who have turned against congregational participation through singing because of their extended bad experiences. The result is a strong backlash and a strongly stated desire to return to the "old" way.

51. Singing in Christian Assemblies in the Earliest Centuries (see p. 57)

There is no doubt whatever that Christian assemblies, from the very origins of the church up to the end of the fifth and the beginning of the sixth centuries, were normally singing assemblies, given the amount and clarity of the historical evidence.

A rigorous study would distinguish between periods and even more between regions. We see that western assemblies, by comparison to regions where there was much singing, such as Syria or North Africa, were slower to follow the impulses of the east; acquired practices were sometimes ephemeral as a consequence of the barbarian invasions, of the end of the *Pax Romana*, and of ancient culture.

It will be useful to recall a number of texts or significant moments.

The earliest evidence goes back to two passages in the Pauline letters: Colossians 3:16 and Ephesians 5:19. These have always been considered as the "rule for singing" in Christian assemblies, from Nicetas of Remesiana[13] or Augustine, Calvin or Coyssard, up to the liturgical reform of Vatican II. Here Paul encourages the existing practice of using different forms of chants, hymns, or songs, as the best way of circulating the word of exhortation and praise among the assembly.

The acclamations and the hymnic elements enshrined in the Book of Revelation in the visions of the heavenly liturgy (e.g., chapters 4 and 5 vv. 8, 11, 12, 13, 14) are obviously inspired by contemporary practice in the Asian Churches.

The celebrated passage in Pliny the Younger to the Emperor Trajan (around the year 114), describing the usages of the Bythinian Christians, indicates a characteristic feature with great precision: the *carmen* (song) that they address to a certain *Chrestos* as if to a God.

In the Christian literature that has come down to us from the first three centuries, hymns hold a prominent place. The evening hymn *Phôs hilaron* and the kernel of the *Gloria in excelsis* go back as far as the second century.[14] Several hundred hymns or fragments of hymns dating back to these earliest centuries were only a very small part of what was created and sung at that time: this helps us to imagine the lyric creativity of the early church.

A major development in singing in the Christian Churches came about in the fourth century, after the Peace of Constantine,

---

13. The authorship of the *Te Deum* is attributed to him.

14. Some have even suggested that the ultimate origin of the *Gloria* is a Delphic hymn to the sun.

with the appearance and diffusion of the responsorial psalm. "A refrain by the whole assembly responds" to verses cantillated at the ambo by a psalmist. This was a real religious and popular event, and this kind of psalm-singing is found with Eusebius in Caesarea, Chrysostom in Antioch or Constantinople, Ambrose in Milan, Nicetas in Remesiana, etc. We can say that at the beginning of the fifth century this practice was almost universal across the Christian world.

Another vein of popular singing that gave birth to an uncountable posterity was the creation of the isosyllabic strophic hymn by Ephrem the Syrian (in Syriac), imitated (in Latin) by Ambrose of Milan in 386, and by a whole host of successors in all sorts of languages right up to our own time.

Among many possible texts, let us cite two passages. The first is taken from an eastern canonical collection of the fourth century:

> The community must respond powerfully to each psalm. If someone is sick and drags behind the rest [?], it is not a fault. But if that person is in good health and remains silent, he or she should be removed. They do not deserve the blessing.
> (Canons of St. Basil)

The second is a passage from St Augustine replying to his disciple Januarius on a number of questions of pastoral practice:

> The only moments when the brethren gathered in the church should not be singing are the readings, the homily, the intentions for prayer, and when the bishop is praying. For the rest of the time, I really do not see that Christians can do anything more useful or holy than sing.
> (Letter 55)

52. Singing "with" (see p. 86)

From the physical point of view, choral singing synchronizes, homogenizes, and stylizes gestural and sonic behavior (pitch, rhythm, dynamic, utterance of a text, etc). As for the symbolic side, what is invested emotionally in each "me" is experienced as a sharing by all the "me"s in the members of the assembly: the "us" of the text is a mere explanation of this "singing with" which is a powerful unison (see GL 58, p. 170). In our civilization it is much less likely that this effect will be produced by a simple listening to music, except under certain conditions which need careful preparation.

53. Solemnity (see p. 34)

In Latin the adjective *solemnis* (or *solennis*) means "something that comes back each year," and thus a consecrated event, celebrated publicly and with a certain sparkle. In the liturgical calendar, Easter—the prime Christian feast—constitutes solemnity par excellence. The other feasts (Christmas, Epiphany, Ascension, Pentecost, and even more the solemnities of the Blessed Virgin Mary and the saints) have no meaning except in relation to Easter. Nevertheless, when talking about solemnity, we should not confuse this word with certain forms of sumptuousness or triumphalism. True solemnity depends on authenticity of expression throughout the liturgical action (see the instruction *Musicam Sacram*, 8 March 1967).

54. Symbol (see pp. 59, 123, 124, and 168)

The notion of symbol can be easily understood through the Greek word from which it derives—the verb *sumbalein*, which means "to gather together"—and through ancient practice: the symbol was a piece (of terracotta, for example) which was broken in two, and then each city in the alliance kept one of the parts. When one of them sent a messenger to the other, they looked to see if the half piece brought by the messenger "fitted together" properly with the piece they had kept: if yes, the messenger really came from the allied town; if not, the messenger was a spy.

The whole of symbol can be found therein. It is a material element (flag, light, music . . .) which allows us to be "gathered together" into a reality which is far from us because it is abstract, or immaterial, or invisible. For example, the flag puts us in the presence of the notion of native land. Light can bring us to the idea of festivity, or life, or glory, or importance, or security, or understanding. Music implants in us the sensation of joy (or sadness), fellowship, communion, festivity, interiorization . . .

We know that liturgy never ceases to work with invisible or immaterial realities (God, grace, prayer, salvation . . .) and so makes the same kind of use of symbolism. But there is a danger here: the symbol is never simply the symbolic object (it is never just the piece broken in two). It is what one does with it—and more than that. It is what happens when we use the object. Bread is not in itself a symbol: it is food. But when we break the bread, it becomes a symbol of sharing and brings us into fraternal life.

(For the higher symbolic value of singing in the liturgy, see GL 58, p. 171)

55. Symbolic Practices (see p. 34)

It is important to emphasize the weight and the force of the word "symbolic" with regard to the liturgical action, in contrast with contemporary language where it refers to actions or attitudes without real value: a symbolic exchange of gifts, or "my participation was merely symbolic."

The word "symbol" has always been used by the church, especially with regard to liturgy, to designate an act, a text, a practice that links the celebrating assembly with something larger than itself (the universal Church), with something other than itself (mystery, grace . . .), and with someone other than itself (the Other: God, the Lord Jesus). And it is precisely this word which is used to indicate the "We believe" through which we profess our faith during the Sunday eucharist: the correct technical term is the Nicaeo-Constantinopolitan Symbol or the Apostles' Symbol (rather than "Creed")—in Latin, *Symbolum*.

In the preceding entry (GL 54, p. 167) a technical explanation of the word "symbol" was given. But the term "symbolic practices" means that no liturgical action closes the celebrating assembly in on itself but, on the contrary, opens the assembly to the mystery of the active presence of the Lord and to communion with the Lord and with the entire body of Christian brothers and sisters spread throughout the world.

Instrumental music and singing, although still being the music and song of a particular assembly and no other, must allow this opening-up and this gathering-together. We will, therefore, be careful to avoid the risk of cozy self-satisfaction that can be generated by the very fact of singing together, and instead substitute a type of instrumental music and a type of singing that are born from within the assembly, whose purpose is not to lead back to the assembly but to lead the assembly beyond itself.

56. Text-Music Relationship, Types of Singing according to the (see p. 71)

We can classify the great variety of types of singing found in the liturgy according to the relationship of the verbal or textual element with the musical element.

According to whether the text or the music predominates, or whether they are balanced, the vocal "gesture" (attitude, posture, both bodily and spiritual) of the singer(s) changes, communication with others (one/all; all/all) is modified, and the rite is more or less meaningful (proclamation, meditation, praise, etc.).

Word ....
.... Music

Spoken language   "Jubilus" vocalises

         Proclamation
        "Cantillation"   Acclamation

        Meditation   Hymn
        Psalmody   "Song"

                Chant
          "verbo-melodism"

N.B. The classification criterion selected here (text-music relationship) is important because it rests on the most characteristic element of Christian worship, namely, the revealed word.

57. Unforeseeable, The (see p. 90)

Except in the case of very large gatherings where the complexity of what is available requires a meticulous observance of the planned chain of events, the most carefully planned order of service must always remain flexible in the manner it is celebrated. If it does not, the celebration runs the risk of becoming totally dehumanized. Liturgy is not something mechanical, nor pure spectacle, but the action of real people relating to each other.

The unforeseen can be simple human error. However carefully you prepare, you should always be ready to cope with incidents along the way. There are two possible frames of mind: either adapt intelligently with an understanding smile, or freeze in a wrathful attitude which destroys communion.

One feast of Epiphany, the priest at the beginning of Mass could not manage to pronounce the name of the feast: "The Eniphapy, I mean the Ephipany—no, the Phenip . . ." The cantor, beaming broadly, launched straight into the refrain of the *Gloria*. The day was saved, and the assembly was bonded together even more closely.

Seriously, though, too rigid an unfolding of the sequence of events can kill the spirit. How can we know in advance how long the silence should be, or how many verses of the opening song will be needed? How can we know if it will feel right to go straight into the psalm after the reading instead of having a silence for reflection? This will depend on the content of the reading, the quality of the reader, and the way in which the assembly welcomes the proclaimed word. So, every minister must be a listener—listening out for God but also listening out for one's sisters and brothers.

If ministers truly enter into this basic frame of mind, even unanticipated changes in the program will be possible: the organist improvising on a well-known refrain brought to mind by the homily; or the cantor at the end of the celebration initiating the reprise of a refrain which seemed to move the assembly in a special way; or even piling up Alleluia upon Alleluia, perhaps because they were rather timidly sung to begin with, or because the context seems to invite this re-sounding repetition.

The unforeseen can also be . . . the unforeseen presence of God.

58. Unison Singing (see pp. 59, 124, 166, and 168)

Unison singing is much richer in meaning than we imagine. "People" gather together and sing a melody together. There are men, women, children, young people, elderly people . . ., people of modest means, others from well-heeled backgrounds . . ., a whole variety of professions, personal histories and family situations . . . Each person has his or her own voice, his or her own timbre . . . Yet, despite this diversity, there is only one melody— there is even only one sound.

Unison singing is the only human phenomenon through which individuals gathered together can create one object perceivable by the senses. People can hold join hands and form a chain: nevertheless, in the visible dimension, it remains quite clear that the individuals have not been "fused" into one. People can talk together, and even speak the same words at the same time: nevertheless, each person speaks in the register of his or her own voice, and there are as many registers as there are participants.

Singing in unison, on the contrary, allows the realization of an entity which "melts" the contribution of each individual personality into a common and unique sonic happening.

Thus we can appreciate the symbolic and even theological importance that unison singing can have in a liturgy which has precisely the goal of uniting all the participating members into one and the same body: the mystical body of Christ. The highest point of expression and realization of this reality occurs at the end of the preface, at the moment when the presider invites the whole assembly to sing the *Sanctus*: "we proclaim your glory by singing with a single voice—*una voce dicentes.*"

(N.B. It goes without saying that this eulogy of unison singing is in no way meant to be a rejection of instrumental or choral polyphony.)

59. "Verbo-Melodism" (see p. 71)

A liturgical chant can never skimp on the coherence between text and music. In this regard musicians who compose for celebration should study the school of Gregorian chant where an exemplary balance between word and melody is realized, and in which the melody is always at the disposal of a word that it serves by giving this word expression, prolongation, and resonance in the celebrating assembly. To evaluate the quality of verbo-melodism, it is necessary to observe the coherence between the movement of the music and that of the text: the correspondence of musical accents with textual accents (isorhythm), the contribution of specific musical processes (acceleration, syncopation, intervals, etc.) to the actualization of the word.

Index to Glossary